From Mummers' P
to Silver Screen

The Life and Times of the Haggar Family

by Vicki Haggar

With contributions from Walter, Roy and Tony Haggar

Edited and compiled by
Linda Asman

Published by Pembroke & Monkton Local History Society
www.pembrokeandmonktonhistory.org.uk

PEMBROKE & MONKTON   LOCAL HISTORY SOCIETY

Supporting
Pembroke Museum

To Merle, with best wishes
Vicki Haggar

Foreword
by Linda Asman

IT WAS through my interest in oral history that I first became acquainted with the Haggar family. When I set out to record the memories of Pembroke people, Roy Haggar was one of the first people I contacted to request an interview. Fortunately, as Haggar is a name that features prominently in Pembroke's past, he agreed to be recorded. It was through Roy, therefore, that I became fully aware of the amazing story of William Haggar, Roy's great grandfather and pioneer of the cinema and film-making in this country.

Part of William's legacy was a chain of family cinemas, one of which was in Pembroke and, although closed down some thirty years ago, still has claims on the affections of a great many people here.

Shortly after this interview, I became interested in digital storytelling as an effective means of conveying local history and I invited a group of people, all of whom I had previously recorded, to make digital stories (short, personal films).

Aided by the professional expertise of Matt White, we worked hard over the following weeks to make the digital stories, one of which was written and narrated by Roy Haggar and which he called *A White Screen and a Good Light;* a lovely, little film which brilliantly encapsulates the Haggar story.

It was a total shock when, just a fortnight later, I was to learn that Roy had suffered a fatal heart attack. I had arranged a social evening for the participants to view their completed digital stories and Roy's sisters Sue, Dinah and Vicki came along.

Vicki and I became close friends and, sharing a love of Pembroke's history, we were founder members of the Pembroke and Monkton Local History Society formed in 2010 to research and promote the history of our historic town. The Society was instrumental in enabling me to pursue the project which had become a passion – to tell the story of Pembroke through the voices of local people in digital stories.

Everyone was enthusiastic about what was to become a community-wide project: a history of Pembroke as seen through the eyes of the people who have lived it. Although carried out voluntarily, an HLF grant enabled publication of *Through My Eyes: a Community History of Pembroke and Monkton* both as a DVD and an accompanying book. It was a big success; people flocked to buy it and I hope it forms something of a memorial to Roy and the Haggars, securing their place in Pembroke's story.

IT WAS always my intention that money raised from the sales of *Through My Eyes* should be put towards publishing further books of local interest and when Vicki consulted with me over her plans to write a book about the Haggar family, I felt this could be something the Society could consider for publication. I am delighted that we have been able to do so.

Although much has been written about William Haggar, Vicki's book takes the story on through four generations of her family and what makes the book unique is that it has been written by members of Vicki's branch of the Haggar family.

Through unpublished essays from the family archive, the story of William Haggar is told both by his great grandson Roy, the family historian, and son Walter who gives us a fascinating eye witness account of those early adventures both in the showing of films in Haggar's travelling cinema or bioscope, then in the making of movies.

From those pioneering days, Vicki continues the story with the setting up of the cinema in Pembroke where her father Len Haggar built up and ran a successful family business for over fifty years.

Haggars Cinema and Ballroom formed the social centre of Pembroke and Vicki, together with her brother Tony, capture the memories of those golden years with contributions from other family members and friends. Eventually Haggars suffered the fate of so many small town cinemas and closed its doors in 1984.

This book, I believe, forms an important chapter in our social history and demonstrates how popular entertainment has evolved over the course of a century, when theatre and cinema were taken to the people in fairgrounds and market places before becoming permanent features in large centres of population.

Going to the pictures featured largely in my young days when every town had at least one cinema. Now those days of the small, family-run cinemas have all but disappeared and a visit to the cinema is not cheap and often means a journey; in South Pembrokeshire there is no cinema at all.

I hope this book will revive some of those memories. It has for me.

Linda Asman
Chairman
Pembroke & Monkton Local History Society

Contents

The Haggar Story
by Vicki Haggar

PART ONE
William Haggar
Pioneer of the British film industry

PART TWO
Haggars in Pembroke

PART THREE
Haggar Remembered

Ornate Bioscope front, built by the Marenghi Company and incorporating a large paper organ actuated by steam. The front was lit by hundreds of coloured bulbs which highlighted the elaborate carved and gilded decoration. The structure was portable but very heavy being built of solid wood. To the modern eye these structures would be more of an attraction than the films shown inside.

Introduction by Vicki Haggar

I WAS born into a remarkable family, a family which has its roots in the Victorian theatre and early cinema. My father was Len Haggar, the well known and respected proprietor of Haggars Cinema and Ballroom in Pembroke and it is there that my earliest memories lie. Alas it is consigned to history.

When the cinema closed in Pembroke in 1984, it represented the end of an era as my family history stretches back through four generations to the very earliest years of the cinema – a history which began with my great grandfather William Haggar, a leading figure in the world of the cinema and pioneer of early film making in this country.

A RTHUR William Haggar was born in Dedham in the Vale of Essex in 1851, the illegitimate son of Elizabeth Haggar. As a young girl, Elizabeth obtained a position in service at the large house of an auspicious family but, during the course of her employment, she fell pregnant; suspicion fell on the son of the house.

Suffice to say that, after the birth of her son and her retire-ment from service, Elizabeth was kept in comfort and eventu-ally became quite a lady living on an income of undisclosed source. Her address in later life was 'Gordon House', Buckley, Kilburn, London. This was to become the business address of William Haggar during his career as a travelling showman.

There do appear to be conflicting versions of William's early years. According to the memoirs of his daughter Lily, William's childhood was not a very happy one, farmed out as he was to various family members and put to work at the age of 12 in his uncle's timber yard.

An alternative version sees him as an 11-year-old appren-tice at a shipyard in Wivenhoe, near Colchester and later apprenticed to a watchmaker. Whatever, his life could not have been easy with little formal schooling and having to work for his living from a very young age.

He did, however, manage something of a musical educa-tion, joining a local band which gave him the opportunity to learn music and play many instruments. He eventually formed a band himself and, at the age of 18, sought his fortune elsewhere. Fortune led him to a company of travelling players, who needed a stage hand with a knowledge of carpentry, and it was not long before William Haggar became an actor and married his leading lady, Sarah Walton, daughter of the company's proprietor.

My great grandmother Sarah must have been a formidable lady and without her William could not have achieved what he did. William and Sarah set up their own company and had eleven children, each one born in a different county of England or Wales: I can only wonder how on earth they managed to bring up such a large family on the road, often enduring considerable hardship.

The first child was William Jnr. who was born in 1871 and was to become an accomplished actor whilst my grandfather Walter, born in 1880, was the fifth child – a natural born leg-puller and comic actor. William and Sarah's other children were: Fred 1873, George 1875-79 (died of smallpox after smallpox vaccination), Ellen 1877-1890 (drowned in the River Wye), Jim 1879, Archie 1882-1894 (died of diphtheria), Rose 1885, Violet 1887, Henry 1889, and Lily May 1891.

THE children were all raised in the world of entertainment and, like their father, were very versatile. Every member of the family could play a musical instrument and between them they could adapt to any role on the stage be it musician, dancer, comedian, actor, singer or compere.

All hands were available when the show needed to be built

William and Sarah Haggar.

up, dismantled and transported to another fairground. William was once asked where he got his actors from and his reply was: 'I breed them Sir'.

It is not my intention to write a detailed history of my great grandfather, William Haggar: his life is well documented elsewhere. Peter Yorke, a great grandson of William, has published a well researched biography which contains a detailed analysis of William Haggar's films, making it an invaluable reference work.

This book, however, tells the story of the life and times of my branch of the Haggar family told through the words and experiences of successive generations.

It opens with the early years of my great grandfather's venture into the world of entertainment: from travelling player to proprietor of a travelling theatre company then bioscope and from film maker to cinema owner. The story continues through four generations and ends with the closing of the last Haggar family cinema in Pembroke.

However, that is not quite the end as Haggars is still remembered in Pembroke with great affection and, in writing this book, it is my intention to preserve the memory.

I have divided the book into three sections. Part One concerns the life and work of William Haggar and was written by my brother Roy and my grandfather Walter in previously

William Haggar's business card with his London address.

unpublished essays. My late, and much-loved brother Roy always cherished our great grandfather's memory and was the family historian, keeper of the flame, giving talks and helping the research of others.

I learnt most of what I know through him and it is fitting, therefore, that the story begins with Roy's short essay on the life and work of William Haggar – a career which began as an actor with a travelling company from which experience sprang his genius as a showman and filmmaker.

In a second essay, Roy takes us back to the theatrical beginnings of the Haggar story, to the trials and tribulations of life in a Victorian travelling theatre company.

The story is continued by my grandfather Walter who tells, first hand, the amazing story of those early pioneering years, experimenting with film and film making, when he was always at his father's side. To anyone interested in the history of the cinema this account represents an invaluable resource but it is, above all, entertaining: Walter's sense of fun and optimism really shines through his writing and I am pleased that this can, at last, be shared by all.

I bring this first section to a close with my own visit to Aberdare, where William Haggar eventually settled and set up his first permanent cinema. The family then went on to establish others, including Haggars of Pembroke which was managed first by Will Haggar Jnr. followed by my grandfather, Walter and then my father, Len Haggar.

This is described in Part Two of the book, which focuses on the Haggar family in Pembroke. Here I have drawn on the memories of my family and local people who affectionately remember Haggars Cinema and Ballroom, for so long the social centre of the town.

I am particularly indebted to my brother Roy's wife Maggie, for permitting the publication of his essays and photographs, and to my brother Tony (Professor Anthony Haggar) who has contributed so much by writing his memories and anecdotes of Haggars in those years when we were young and involved in it all. And thanks also go to my close friend and companion James Spooner for his invaluable help and support.

In the third and concluding part I have looked at William Haggar's enduring legacy, his place in cinema history and the efforts we are making locally to celebrate his life and work.

Yes, the name Haggar is very much remembered in Pembroke and I hope this book will be welcomed by people not only in Pembroke but by all those interested in the history of the cinema.

I WAS encouraged to write this book through my involvement with the Pembroke & Monkton Local History Society, which is dedicated to preserving the memory of times past in Pembroke and I thank the Committee for agreeing to publish it. I am indebted also to the present Chairman of the Society, Linda Asman, for her contribution to the book and for her assistance in editing it.

Acknowledgements:

National Sound and Film Archive of Wales, National Library Wales at Aberystwyth; National Library of Wales, Newspapers on-line: the *Aberdare Leader;* Pembrokeshire Archives and Local Studies; The Bill Douglas Museum, Exeter; Denise Price of Aberdare Library; BBC Wales; *Pembrokeshire Life* article on the Palace Cinema in Pembroke Dock by Keith Johnson; *Western Telegraph; West Wales Guardian*; *Wales and the Cinema – The First Hundred Years* by David Berry.

PART ONE
William Haggar
Pioneer of the British Film Industry

Chapter 1

William Haggar – His Life in Brief by Roy Haggar

'Vision is the art of seeing things invisible'
Jonathan Swift

WILLIAM Haggar was born in the Vale of Dedham, Essex in 1851. Apprenticed as a shipwright and later as a watchmaker, he became an accomplished musician and joined a travelling theatre company. He married Sarah Walton, daughter of its proprietor, Richard Walton, in 1870.

The Waltons had been actors and entertainers for generations and William embarked with the theatre on a new apprenticeship as a comic actor. The couple were very much in love and to prove it they had eleven children, each one born in a different county of England or Wales. All these children were brought up to the profession of the stage.

The wanderings of the family brought them in 1890 to Chepstow on the borders of Wales and there, tragically, their eldest daughter Nell was drowned in the River Wye. They moved on with the theatre into the coal valleys of Wales which brought them an unprecedented level of prosperity.

At this time William Haggar became the proprietor of the theatre and continued the tour into industrial Wales and the agrarian west, where they eventually visited Pembroke. The Welsh people in the more remote towns and villages in Wales warmly welcomed the theatre with its repertoire of over a hundred stock Victorian melodramas and comedies. The most popular play, everywhere in Wales, was the old folk story *The Maid of Cefn Ydfa*.

During this period William embarked on another apprenticeship as a photographer. He acquired a plate camera and, after much experiment, he set himself up as a professional photographer in a portable studio next to the theatre; not only would he take his patrons' photographs, he would frame them.

In 1897 William Haggar was standing with the Castle Theatre in Aberavon. Business was good, as the new docks were being built at that time, and William had saved up £80.00. He had become fascinated by the new phenomena of moving pictures and he spent his savings purchasing a projector and a few films.

He built a small ground booth which he named The Windsor Castle Theatre, and set off with his young sons to Aberavon Fair where, for the first time, he attempted to show moving pictures to the public on 5th April 1898. Once he had overcome people's reluctance to pay for something they had never heard of, he did good business taking £15.00 in pennies on the first night. As he counted the cash he looked at his sons and said: "I knew there was money in it."

William handed the Castle Theatre over to his son William Jnr. and his wife Jenny Lindon and began a new career as proprietor of a travelling picture show (the Bioscope). This daring venture brought the family close to starvation. 1898 saw the great coal strike in South Wales: there were few pennies around for travelling picture shows.

Even in the agrarian counties the public quickly tired of the novelty of moving pictures. They were what showmen call 'oncers', as people would only pay once to see what were rather repetitive pictures. Haggar restored his fortunes with a successful winter tour of South Wales with the pantomime *Cinderella*. He realised that if the Bioscope were to be a permanent success it would need a more extensive repertoire; unfortunately the best films were French and very expensive.

Right: William Haggar showed an early interest in photography with his own portable studio. This is a portrait photograph of his daughter Lily.

W. *Haggar*, Photographer, CASTLE THEATRE STUDIO

When a competitor, Harry Scard, filmed and exhibited a Wales v England football match, William was galvanised into action; he suddenly saw the way forward. William went to London and visited the Gaumont Company where he bought a camera and film, determined to make his own pictures.

He had certain advantages. He had spent a lifetime in the theatrical profession; possessed the services of a stock company with actors, plays, costumes and sets; he was a skilled photographer and, most important, he was a showman who knew how to entertain his audiences.

THE experiment began in 1901 with a short film of a train entering Burry Port Station and he followed this with a series of short incident films including *A Phantom Ride through Swansea*, *Patrick Pinches Poultry*, a film of the Russo-Japanese war and a film of the Boer War taken in the Rhymney Valley.

Haggar was learning and, in 1902, he and his sons Walter and Jim took their camera up the valley to Maesteg where William Jnr. was standing with the Castle Theatre. A family conference ensued and it was decided to make a film of *The Maid of Cefn Ydfa*.

William Haggar, Showman.

This melodrama was an old favourite of Welsh audiences and it had the advantage that the story was well known; the play of the film would only need to be approximate.

A stage was set up in the sunlight, the actors quickly rehearsed and the film was shot in seven scenes in little more than an hour and a half. Additional action scenes were set in the hills around Maesteg and the film was completed.

Also in this year 1902, Haggar made the classic, horror silent films *True as Steel* ('a sensational fight between a knight and a forest hermit') and *The Maniac's Guillotine*.

Again, William Haggar used his family as the cast and the films were shown at his fairground bioscope.

The Maid was first shown at Treorchy Fair and in modern terms it was a sensation – the Welsh people flocked to see it. *The Maid* literally made William Haggar's fortune.

It was probably the first British film that related to its audience in a regional sense and it lived on in the collective folk memory of the people of South Wales until comparatively recent times.

This success was followed by many films including *A Desperate Poaching Affray* which sold over 480 copies in Europe and the U.S.A., *The Sign of the Cross*, *The Life of Charles Peace*, *The Dumb Man of Manchester*, *Maria Marten*, *A Message from the Sea*, *The Women of Mumbles Head* and the *Mirthful Mary* and the *Weary Willie and Tired Tim* series.

In 1912 another version of *The Maid* was filmed which ran for 50 minutes, a remarkable length for its time.

By 1914 the Haggar family had made more than sixty films and William Haggar had established himself as one of the true pioneers of film making in Britain.

The success of these films brought prosperity and the Bioscope became the foremost attraction at the British fairground. It was the era of steam, of the great traction engines and the elaborate gaudy organ fronts.

Roy Haggar with a portrait of William Haggar. Picture: Gareth Davies

Alas the hey-day of the Bioscope was short and it was all finished by the Great War in 1914. By the time the conflict was over the cinema had settled into permanent halls in towns and cities throughout the United Kingdom.

The Haggars had bought The Royalty Theatre in Llanelli in 1910, The Rink in Pontardulais in 1912 and these were followed by cinemas in Aberdare, Neath, Mountain Ash and Pembroke. The cinema had become an institution and the British and French film producers who had led the way were eclipsed by the economic power of Hollywood.

Chapter 2
Early Years in the Travelling Theatre by Roy Haggar

DURING the closing years of the nineteenth century and the early years of the twentieth century the travelling players with their portable theatre – the descendants of the mummer's booth – was a familiar phenomenon both in the prosperous industrial towns and valleys and in the more remote agricultural regions of South Wales.

The theatres flourished along with the chapels most probably for a similar reason; that they allowed the Welsh people a limited expression for the love of music and drama which is characteristic of the race and had been stultified by the depressing forces of the industrial revolution.

It is doubtful if the ministers of religion approved of the actors. To the puritanical they must have seemed a danger to the morals of the community but, although their motives were dissimilar, there is little doubt that they were to some extent fulfilling a similar need in the bleak mining valleys and lonely agricultural towns and hamlets of south Wales.

There were several companies touring in Wales at this time: Jackson's Victoria Theatre, Edward Ebley's Palace of Varieties and Johnny Noakes, who settled in Aberdare with his portable theatre for two years and who was later to build the Royalty Theatre in Llanelli. Here, however, I am concerned with only one of these companies, that of my family the Haggars, and to illustrate from their experience the life, techniques and itinerary of a company of travelling players in South Wales during the period.

WILLIAM Haggar joined Richard Walton's Travelling Theatre Company and married his leading lady, Sarah Walton, in 1871. Sarah's family had been in theatricals as long as anyone could remember and she was reputed to be capable of playing any of the women's parts in Shakespeare without rehearsal.

She trained her new husband as a comic actor and during the years that followed they travelled throughout Great Britain playing in portable and permanent theatres, and in their spare time producing a family of eleven children, all of whom were reared to the stage.

William and Sarah initially toured the south western counties of England. This area was in the grip of the agricultural depression of the eighties and nineties; business was poor and often the actors' existence was barely above starvation level. They played in the towns of the area including Dorchester, Poole, Romsey, Andover, Winchester and Swindon but the audiences were so sparse that the Company was eventually forced to disband.

William Haggar, with a young family to support, carved himself a number of puppets and attempted to make for his family and himself a living on the local fairgrounds. The puppets, however, were little more successful than the live theatre.

In 1888 William and Sarah rejoined the Company in the town of Thornbury, where business improved. Via Gloucester and Chepstow, the Company moved gradually toward South Wales and in the summer of 1889 the theatre was built up in Ebbw Vale, where the business was so good that they were able to stay for the unprecedented time of six months.

The Travelling Theatre

THE THEATRE was, of necessity, portable and was, as is suggested by its alternative name of 'Fit-Up', a prefabricated affair of wooden frames, boards, flats, canvas and rope. The stage consisted of two flat trucks run together with a proscenium built around them.

The front of the theatre was built up of two living wagons set apart with a small front stage or 'parade' built between.

On each side of the living wagons were steps leading into the theatre known as the 'Walk Up'. The sides and roof of the theatre were constructed of frames carrying wooden panels and the whole covered with a canvas tilt pegged down firmly with guys and stakes. The seating capacity was in the region of two hundred and the seats were bare boards running down to the stage.

The theatre was sited wherever a pitch could be obtained and, if fortunate, this would be on a site within the town such as a square or market place or, if less fortunate, in a field on the outskirts of the town.

Both theatre and business were at the mercy of the elements: a wet and stormy night in a South Wales mining valley could mean an empty house. On one occasion in Abertillery, the whole company were up six days and nights preventing the theatre from blowing down.

In the same place, the actors were in the middle of a morning rehearsal on a beautiful, sunny day when the whole structure was blown to the ground by a freak gust of wind. As the theatre had been erected in a sheltered spot in the valley the actors had neglected to guy the structure down with stakes!

The gentlemen of the Company had not only to be actors, but also carpenters, labourers, painters and Jacks of all trades. They had to build the theatre manually and keep it in good repair; then they had to dismantle, transport and erect the structure on its various sites. If the theatre was damaged by a gale, as it was at Abertillery, they had to set-to and rebuild it.

The Haggar family at the wedding of Walter and Ada who are standing in the centre of the photograph. Seated left are Jenny Lindon, William and Sarah. Standing behind are Will Junior, Lily and Violet.

As the Company became more prosperous, they built themselves more elaborate theatres. The most elegant was the new Castle Theatre, the front of which consisted of flats painted to resemble a castle gaily decorated with flags and bunting, with the actors on the parade dressed in military uniforms.

During the time of the Boer War the actors were dressed in contemporary uniform and the actresses as nurses: the song of the day was, of course, *Goodbye Dolly Gray*.

Scenery and props were painted and constructed by the men of the Company. For the more popular plays, stock scenery was kept and transported but, for a new play, appropriate scenery would be painted and any furniture, drapes or props made by members of the Company.

In the early days, lighting the stage was by oil lamp and dimming effects obtained by sliding semi-transparent paper in front of the footlights. Later, naphtha, acetylene and limelight were used. With the advent of electricity, power for lighting was generated by the use of a portable gas or petrol driven engine which enabled the use of spots and flood lighting.

The Haggar Company playbill for The Royal, Chepstow.

THEATRE ROYAL,
THE MEADS, CHEPSTOW.

TUESDAY, APRIL 29th, 1890.

SPECIAL PERFORMANCE
UNDER THE PATRONAGE & PRESENCE OF
MAJOR JAMES FOTHERGILL EVANS,
And OFFICERS commanding the 1st Detachment 2nd Volunteer Battalion South Wales Borderers;
Dr. E. P. KING & ROBERT CLIVE, Esq.
On which occasion the Performance will commence with
THE SPARKLING COMEDY,
ENTITLED:

"The Test of Truth."

RODERICK PRAISEWORTHY	-	MR. HENRY C. SELBY
THEODORE PRODIGAL } his nephews	"	W. HAGGAR, JUN.
REGINALD PRODIGAL }	"	HORACE R. MAIR
	"	W. HAGGAR, SEN.
CAPIAS SHARKE	"	H. BLANDFORD
MAJOR STORMONT	"	F. HAGGAR
BUTTONS	"	L. NANTON.
WHIPCORD	-	MISS M. ASKEY
MARY	-	MRS. H. R. MAIR
SUSAN	-	W. HAGGAR
MADAME REGINALD PRODIGAL	-	MISS ALICE LATIMER
ELLEN PRODIGAL		

Songs - - Mr. W. HAGGAR, Sen.

TO CONCLUDE WITH
THE CELEBRATED LAUGHABLE FARCE,
ENTITLED:
'THE QUEER FAMILY'

RESERVED SEATS, 2/-; FRONT SEATS, 1/-; PIT, 6d.
DOORS OPEN AT 7.15; PERFORMANCE TO COMMENCE AT 7.45 P.M. PROMPT.
CARRIAGES MAY BE ORDERED FOR 10.15.

ENOCH WILLIAMS, PRINTER, CHEPSTOW.

The ladies of the Company made any costumes, drapes, wigs or masks required. Large stocks of these were carried but a new play would require a visit to one of the larger towns for the purchase of material, buttons, lace and satins.

Greasepaint was generally used for make-up. When money was short any material that was suitable for the job would be used.

In an attempt to satisfy the contemporary demand for realism on stage, the Company contrived to produce as realistic and spectacular effects as possible within their limited means. Thunder was produced with the time-honoured aid of a large piece of tin, and dried peas poured upon the same simulated the effect of heavy rain. Snow could be made by using paper confetti or, as on one occasion at a Christmas pantomime, goose feathers.

Strong wind was produced with the aid of a hand operated wind machine and smoke by the simple but dangerous and uncomfortable expedient of burning damp rags in a brazier. It was with sets and props, however, that they attempted to give the illusion of reality and, apparently, these were skilfully and accurately painted.

The theatre was transported on three flat trucks: costumes, props and scenery were loaded onto two box wagons which

Three of Haggar's sons, Walter, Archie and Henry.

could also serve as living quarters. Teams of horses would be hired to pull the wagons to the next town.

The length of stay on any one site would depend on the quality of business, but it was never less than a week and might be as long as eighteen months.

Will Junior and Jenny Lindon's Company.

When the time came to move on, the theatre was dismantled and loaded onto wagons following the final Saturday evening performance, ready for departure. A move usually took a week to complete and the theatre would be reassembled and ready for opening on the following Saturday night.

Actors were paid under what was known as the share or 'Commonwealth' system. The takings were divided into equal shares and each member of the company would receive a number of shares depending on his status, or position.

At the end of the evening performance, the pianist would count the takings and, when this had been balanced with the ticket counterfoils, the shares would be announced to the eagerly awaiting Company: 'shares nine pence' or 'shares three pence'.

The leading man, comedian and villain would receive a share and a half, the leading lady a share and a quarter and the supporting players, one share. Four shares would be put aside for the maintenance of the theatre, two for travelling expenses and two for sundries such as gas cylinders and material for props and costumes.

*Will Junior and
Jenny Lindon.*

The Repertoire

THE performance would consist of a play, a comic or farcical sketch, a couple of comic songs and possibly a tableaux of either one of the more dramatic scenes of the play or a topical item of contemporary news.

The Company had a repertoire of stock plays including the Victorian melodramas *East Lynne*, *Uncle Tom's Cabin*, *Maria Marten*, *Sweeny Todd*, *The Cross Roads of Life*, *Ingomar the Barbarian*, *The Sign of the Cross*, *The Silver King*, *Ten Nights in a Bar Room*, *Trilby*, *The Maid of Cefn Ydfa* and *Hoodman Blind*. To avoid the payment of copyright fees the titles of the plays would be slightly altered: *The Silver King* would be billed as *The Silver Ring*, *The Sign of the Cross* as *The Shadow of the Cross* and *The Dumb Man of Manchester* as *The Mute of Manchester*.

Many of the stock plays could be staged and performed at a moment's notice. The play for the opening night was always *The Crossroads of Life*; repetitive performances ensured that the play was 'stage ready', the business of the move allowing no time for adaptation or rehearsal.

The Company was capable of and often did present a fresh play every night. For this reason the players were type-cast and their roles stayed with them: villain, hero, heroine or comedian. Their knowledge of the parts was necessary to their trade and the morning rehearsal at eleven o'clock was sufficient preparation for a faultless performance in the evening!

One of the disadvantages of this type of casting was that the audience associated a player's role with his character in actual life. Will Haggar Jnr., who at the time was cast as the villain, was once attacked in the streets of Llanelli by an old lady with a gamp who berated him as a drunken womaniser. Rising to the part he stood to his full six feet two inches and in his best stage voice replied: "Madam at least you will never have the good fortune to become one of my victims, good day."

WILLIAM Haggar was the comedian of the Company and in South Wales he had the nickname of 'Haggar Out'. He earned this on one occasion in Tredegar, when a new comedian was given a trial.

This unfortunate was hissed from the stage and a cry went up from the audience 'Send Haggar Out, Send Haggar Out' and the name stuck to him throughout his subsequent career on the stage. An unfortunate result of this reputation was that he was unable (much to his chagrin, for he was a very versatile actor) to play any other role.

An attempt to play a heavy part was sufficient to reduce an audience to hysterics. On one occasion, due to the absence of an actor, he played the villain in *Maria Marten*. Fortunately the original actor returned the next day for, as it was said in the Company, 'This was the only time *Maria* was played as a comedy'.

The Company's library of plays consisted, in the main, of hand-written scripts. If a new play were to be added to the repertoire, one printed copy was obtained and handed around. Each member of the cast would copy out and learn his part.

Even a new play would merit no more than three or four rehearsals and could be performed without the need for prompting or gagging.

Actors had their own speciality acts which were usually performed following the main play. William Haggar had a repertoire of over a hundred comic songs and monologues including many of the contemporary Dan Leno successes.

Dick Walton's speciality was a spectacular two-handed sword fight. Holding a cutlass in each hand he would, with considerable expertise, engage in a duel and defeat six opponents.

A favourite speciality of the Company was a fencing duel between six ladies and a similar number of gentlemen, which was performed with formal and precise movement to a musical accompaniment.

Music was an integral part of any performance; besides the piano, there was a band of up to eight instrumentalists. This musical accompaniment was in later years provided by the Haggar children, each of whom could play one or more instruments.

Playbill for a production by Will Junior and Jenny Lindon.

1823

To record

Murder

This Stone was erected over the body of

Margaret Williams

Aged 26

A native of Carmarthenshire, being in service in this Parish, who was found dead, with marks of violence upon her person, in a ditch on the Marsh below the Churchyard, on the morning of Sunday, July 1822.

Although

The Savage Murderer

escaped for a season—the detection of man—

God hath set a mark upon him

either for time or eternity, and

The Cry of Blood

will assuredly pursue him to certain and terrible, but righteous

Judgment.

Canys nyni a adwaenom y neb a ddywedodd, Myfi biau dial, myfi a delaf, medd yr Arglwydd. A thrachefn, Yr Arglwydd a farna ei bobl.— HEB. X., 3p

The above is the correct wording on the Stone in Cadoxton Churchyard to be seen to-day and upon which a splendid Welsh Drama has been written, and will be played by

Will Haggar & Miss Jenny Lindon's
Select Players.

It was a dictum of the Company that the audience should leave the theatre laughing and the performance always concluded with a comic sketch or song to relieve the tensions created by the Victorian melodrama.

Each Christmas the Company would prepare and stage a pantomime. This meant weeks of preparatory work involving the writing of a script, the learning of songs, making scenery, costumes and wigs. The pantomime was performed for a week only and, apparently, there was little profit in the venture.

However, it became something of a ritual and every year, without fail, the actors produced this show with the greatest enthusiasm and enjoyment.

In the words of a member of the family 'It was purely for the love of the game'.

William Haggar, travelling player, with two-year-old Violet.

24

The Company of Actors

A COMPANY of actors consisted of about eight men, four women, wives and children. Each person, even if not acting, was involved in the theatre in some capacity such as seamstress, utility man, scene painter or musician.

The children of course were reared to the profession, beginning behind the scenes and graduating to walk-on juvenile parts and finally as actors in their own right. Their formal education was, due to the nature of their way of life, sketchy. Their real education was the stage.

As I have previously described, the actors of the portable theatre had to play many parts not only on stage but off, and their existence was precarious and often uncomfortable. The constant movement, search for cheap lodgings (which varied in quality), hard work, late nights, early mornings and the occasional descent into near penury does little to suggest a life of glamour.

Their audiences, although usually appreciative, could be rough, particularly in times of social or industrial disturbance. Before and during a performance a little handbell would be rung to bring the audience to order. If, after repeated applications, this had no effect the actors would descend from the stage and forcibly eject any hooligans. They would then return to the stage and, with apologies to the audience, continue with the play.

On one occasion, during a big mining strike in the valleys, a crowd of angry colliers turned their attention to the theatre and, after stoning the actors, threatened to burn it down. The situation was only saved by one of the more courageous of the Company who jumped up on the parade and, after delivering a tremendous oration on the grievances and misfortunes of the working man, managed to get them singing.

THESE people were professionals and it can only have been the love of the life which persuaded them to follow the theatre. Their twin consolations were found in their performances and drink and often the two would become inextricably mingled.

After a performance, with their shares in their pockets, the actors would retire to the local tavern and regale their colleagues, and anyone else willing to listen, with details of their performances past and present. If the shares were high, the more profligate of the cast might be permanently drunk; often a hurried search of the local hostelries had to be undertaken before, or even during, a performance.

On one occasion in Tonypandy, the leading man, a powerful actor named Clarence Mangau, was missing prior to the beginning of a performance. One of the Haggar sons was dispatched to his lodgings only to find him drunk in bed. Mangau, realising the purpose of the visit, bared his breast and in his best dramatic manner cried:

"Walter! Walter! Do you think I would contaminate my fellow players? No! Look at me – smallpox! I can't possibly leave this room for weeks. Go! Go! Tell them they will see me in Heaven."

With this proclamation he fell sobbing into his bed. Walter, in a high state of excitement, rushed back to the theatre with his terrible news only to be received by his unsympathetic father who, familiar with Mangau's wiles, guessed the truth.

Walter had further cause to regret the actor's intemperance as he was pushed onto the stage to play the part; one of the few occasions when a prompter was required.

In the town of Dorchester the three Loydall brothers – actors associated with the Haggar family for many years – were drinking in an inn at lunch time when they became involved in a fight with two soldiers. Fleeing the pub, they ran into two more soldiers whom they punched on the nose and so on up the street.

That evening, the audience in the theatre consisted entirely of the military, with belts and boots at the ready, awaiting the appearance of the Loydall brothers. In the interests of their own safety and that of the theatre, it was decided that it would be advisable if the Loydalls did not appear; they were smuggled out of the town hidden in a horse-drawn cart!

It was escapades such as these, and the almost impossible task of imposing discipline on the Company when the shares were high, which resulted in the abandonment of the Commonwealth system.

When the Company entered Wales and William Haggar became the proprietor of the theatre, he employed his actors to impose more control. This did not entirely cure the trouble, however, and he continued to suffer considerable mortification at the hands of temperamental actors and actresses.

There was often considerable professional jealousy between the players. At one rehearsal, while an actress was singing the song *That is Love* another of the ladies entered the theatre and indignantly cried: 'My song, darling.'

This was met with the retort 'What do you mean your song?'

A female fracas ensued which ended with the unfortunate proprietor having to sing the song himself.

Friction was also created by the casting of speciality parts. During the casting of *Trilby*, for example, Clarence Mangau wished to play Svengali, although he was not as suitable for the part as a Mr. George Butler, who had played the role previously with great success.

A serious argument ensued between the two concerning their various merits for the role and it took great tact to mollify Mangau and to assign the role to Butler. This achieved, the play was subsequently a great success.

There is little doubt that the actors and actresses of the portable theatre were as temperamental and demonstrative as their more salubrious and well known contemporaries and descendants.

They were, however, well loved and respected by their

Violet Haggar.

audiences and achieved, in South Wales at least, a local and, what must have been for them, a gratifying fame. Their acting was, apparently, in the typical Victorian style with exaggerated facial, bodily and vocal gestures. This did not detract from the enjoyment of the unsophisticated audiences of the day, however, and they were sufficiently involved to warn the heroine of her inevitable fate, to hiss and boo the villains and to cod the comedians.

The performance was not always without incident. On one occasion Haggar was in the middle of a particularly moving love scene when a youth in the wings dropped the tabs.

The infuriated actor castigated the boy in unwholesome language and the terrified unfortunate promptly raised the tabs again, presenting the audience with the sight and sound of the lover hurling obscenities into the wings. On realising what had happened, he stopped, looked at his audience and without a flicker of emotion gathered his swooning lady into his arms and reverted to his role. This performance brought the house down.

THE COMPANY entered Wales in 1891 and, after a stay of six months at Ebbw Vale, their subsequent itinerary was to take them throughout the southern part of the Principality.

Following the stay at Ebbw Vale they visited Tredegar, Brynmawr, Abertillery and Tonypandy where they stayed for 18 months. In 1896 they visited Llanelli where business was so poor that they moved into the Rhondda Valley.

A saying grew up amongst the Company at this time 'stick to the coal'. This was apparently good advice as the colliers and their families were always the most appreciative and affluent of their audiences.

During this period a second theatre was built and placed under the management of Will Haggar Jnr. This began another circuit playing at Pontypool, Cwmbran, Blaenavon and finishing at Ton Pentre during the Diamond Jubilee in 1897.

In the same year the two Companies rejoined at Aberavon but business was so poor that the theatre was loaded onto its trucks and the Company departed on a tour of West Wales which lasted for thirteen weeks, playing in the small towns of Pembrokeshire and Carmarthenshire.

In 1898 the Company returned to Aberavon where they found the place bustling with the work of building the new Margam Docks. The tour in West Wales having been successful financially, the Company built a new theatre, the Castle Theatre, which was an immediate success.

Other ventures were also sponsored at this time: Haggar's Pavilion, the Star Palace of Varieties and the Theatre Pavilion. These were managed by other members of the family but did not have the complete success of the Castle Theatre.

The Demise of the Travelling Theatre

IN 1899 William Haggar and his son Walter left the theatre to experiment with the new phenomena of moving pictures and Will Haggar Jnr. and his wife Jenny Lindon, the daughter of an old acting family, continued to tour with the Castle.

This final tour lasted from 1899 until 1916 and many seasons were played in the Welsh towns including Caerphilly and Abergavenny (1904), Mountain Ash, Ferndale, Neath, (1908-10); Pontardawe, Bargoed and Fochriw (1913-14) and Pontlottyn.

By 1916, however, the live theatre was dying in the face of competition from films and with great reluctance the theatre was converted into a cinema.

The Castle Theatre in Pontlottyn was burned down in 1914 when a petrol generating set exploded giving the waiting crowds its final and probably most spectacular performance.

More serious, however, was a subsequent fire at Pontardulais in 1923 when the Castle's successor was gutted. Not only was the cinema destroyed, but also the whole stock in trade of the theatrical profession – scenery, costumes, manuscripts and printed copies of the dramas and comedies which had been the basis of the family's profession on the stage.

William Haggar had to be held back to prevent him entering the flames in an attempt to rescue these items. He probably realised that what was being burned was not only the cinema and the tools of his acting profession, but also a way of life.

He had little respect for what he contemptuously referred to as 'the celluloid actors' and survived this disaster by only a few years.

Chapter 3
The Bioscope Era by Walter Haggar

MARKET place, Aberavon, Sept 1897; this is the date when my father Mr. William Haggar Senior acquired a cinematograph. He was a subscriber to a photographic periodical called *Focus* and in this there were several technical articles dealing with animated photography, and its use and application for various purposes including entertainment.

The first animated photographic instrument that Father saw was called a Kinetoscope, a penny-in-the-slot machine in which a film could be seen through a peep-hole viewer. The first animated pictures he saw on the screen were at the Empire, Cardiff in the early spring of 1898.

At this period, the Empires of Messrs. Moss Empires Ltd. at Cardiff, Swansea and Newport were showing a variety of animated pictures, which I thought very good. It had been suggested that Mr. William Haggar Snr. was the first to show animated pictures in Wales; this is not so.

It was nearing the end of our portable theatre days when we were pitched at Aberavon Market Place with the Castle Theatre. This was at the time of the construction of the Margam Dock and Aberavon was teeming with labourers with the result that we had a very good season there.

But the eccentricities of actors and actresses employed by my father during the whole of his entertainment life were more than enough for any man to tolerate so, upon reading of the possibilities of animated pictures as an entertainment, he decided to make a change.

As I heard him say on more than one occasion, he could put his actors to bed in their little tin boxes each night and know that they were available and sober for the entertainment next day.

One day, whilst reading his publication *Focus*, Mr Haggar saw an advertisement for the sale of a cinematograph and triunial lantern including the gas cylinders, regulators, cages, lantern slides, films etc., the whole for £80. Away went Mr. Haggar to Exeter and came back with the whole outfit, all agog with excitement and very nearly broke because £80 in those days was a lot of money – and it was a cash transaction paid in gold.

Haggar's Royal Electric Bioscope 1902. This was Haggar's first travelling bioscope. It was a self- build show and painted on the entrance doors were the topical figures of the Boer War heroes, General Roberts and Kitchener. The show was built up between two wagons and the frontage displayed an 87 key Gavioli Fairground Organ. Lighting was provided by the steam-powered generator which was mostly hidden behind decorative front panels.

The experiment

THE MOST important thing in this equipment was the Instruction Book – and if any of the modern operators in their exclusive Odeon or Gaumont Cinemas think it was easy, fifty years ago, to undertake to learn to operate a gas illuminated cinematograph with no personal instruction, relying only on an instruction book, let them try it! I should like to point out that Mr. William Haggar, my father, was an actor with a portable theatre who had never seen or handled a gas cylinder.

The light to project films in those days was limelight; this comprised two gases, oxygen and hydrogen under pressure in cylinders. These gases would impinge on the lime (the lime being a circle about the size of a cotton reel) and the result was a brilliant white light known as limelight.

My father arrived from Exeter with the new outfit and with the aid of my brother, Mr James Haggar, erected it on the stage behind the backdrop. They patted and fondled it, and then had to take it down and put it back in its cases as it was time for opening the theatre.

Repeat performance next day, having another look at it. On the third or fourth day, with the aid of the Instruction Book they pursued a little further.

"What did the Instruction Book say?" (Father)

"First turn on the hydrogen – the red tab. Have you got the cylinder key?"

"Here it is Dad."

"Right, turn on the hydrogen – red cylinder. Have you got the Instruction Book? What is next?"

"Light the hydrogen on a low gas."

"Got a match?"

"No, Dad."

Out went Jim for a match. During all this time the lantern which housed the limelight was being filled with that highly combustible coal gas, hydrogen. When Jim finally arrived back with the matches, they applied one to this miniature bomb. Result 'Bang!' and panic.

Shouts of "Shut off the cylinders!" Palpitating hearts, utter darkness, then – "What did you do?"

"I only applied a match!"

"Where's the Instruction Book?" said Father, his chest almost bursting with fear. "What did you do?"

"Nothing, I only struck the match," said Jim.

"Let's try again, give me the book. Now then, what do we do? Turn on the coal gas - don't turn it on so highly! Have you got a match ready? You hold the match to the lime and I will turn the cylinder gently."

The gas alighted and, according to the Book, it had to remain alight a little while to warm the lime preparatory to turning on the other gas, oxygen.

"Where is the cylinder key?"

"Here you are, Dad, what are you going to do?"

"The Instruction Book says turn on the other cylinder."

On went number two which, being of high pressure, blew the pipe at each end causing a repetition of panic, further palpitations of the heart and packing up the entire outfit for that day, and a very close study of the Instruction Book for further details.

A WEEK elapsed, more mundane details requiring immediate attention – the advertising of the dramatic performances – had to take their place.

However, they were not daunted by their two panics, although they were getting very much afraid by now.

But like good pioneers (and having paid £80 for the outfit) there was nothing left but to get on with it. So rehearsal number three took place.

This time they took the precaution of warming the gas pipes to ensure that they did not blow under pressure; it was getting obvious that these gases were under pressure and as such had to be controlled.

Very well, out came the inevitable Instruction Book at the same page. They turned on the hydrogen gently, lit it, let it warm up and gently turned on the oxygen.

Now, before going any further, I must explain that in the limehouse there was what was known as a jet with two taps, two nipples to take these cylinder connections and a mixing chamber for the gases to mix, come out of the jet and impinge on the lime in the proper proportions to get a good light.

It is certainly much more difficult to operate and get a good light by limelight than it is with the modern projection elements.

Walter and Lily Haggar as Charles Peace and Accomplice.

After various attempts, they got a good light and projected it onto the screen. This took them nearly a fortnight and they were quite elated to get such a good light; they even went so far as to turn the cinematograph handle to see the thing flicker.

I MENTIONED earlier that the outfit was a Triunial. This meant that there were three lanterns, one on top of the other. The two top lanterns were for slides.

Why two? There was in those days what is known as 'dissolving views' i.e. you showed one lantern slide and the second slide was shown on the same screen with increasing light power, number one having a decreasing light power. When one view faded away, the other view took its place with a very pleasing effect known as a dissolving view, and this was quite a feature in this type of entertainment in those days.

The dissolving was achieved with the limelights; the two lantern slides were in their carriers behind the lenses, a brilliant light behind one, a by-pass only behind the other and the dissolving effect was achieved by inducing the light from number one lantern into number two softly and gently, which gave the aforementioned pleasing effect.

These two lanterns were mounted above the lantern which housed the light for the cinematograph proper, which was on the 'bottom floor', shall we say. Needless to say there was quite a maze of taps and pipes and fittings etc., to be attended to by the operator.

After weeks of experimenting with the aid of the Instruction Book and, with a great deal of perseverance, they were able to run a film. Included in the outfit from Exeter were 13 or 14 films of different lengths; 50 ft, 75 ft and 100 feet. There were no reels, no spools, just a naked film and, incidentally, they were of the identical width and size that are running today.

In fact, the principal of the cinematograph remains unchanged during the last fifty years. It is a series of photographs shown in rapid succession on a screen. But films fifty years ago were, as said, 50 ft, 75 ft or 100 ft – one foot per second.

We had *The Turn-out of the London Fire Brigade*, *A Boxing Match*, *Loie Fuller Dancing*, *Train Emerging from a Tunnel* etc. I remember one gentleman saying to my father: "All you want to complete your set of films is a rough sea."

Try to visualise, whoever reads this, that in those days acted films were never thought of; one had an animated picture camera and anything that was animated was the subject of a film.

There were no spool boxes in those days and, by the way, no licensing requirements. These short films were threaded onto a reel, run through the machine, and run loose into an open-mouthed bag, but how the devil you found the ends to rewind them is nobody's business.

Experience soon taught us that the films should not be allowed to run loose into the linen bag. The beginning did not matter, that went into the bag all right, but as the end left the machine it was carefully grabbed and pinned to the side of the linen bag, and was easily found for re-winding.

We were progressing, getting more experience and we were now confident enough to invite the local doctor, the vicar and one or two friends to a private exhibition of our latest acquisition of the entertainment world, the cinematograph.

One safety device of this particular cinematograph was a shallow alum bath interposing between the limelight and the inflammable film. A depth of half an inch of alum water was reputed to remove the danger of fire. Unfortunately our alum bath had a slow heat and on the particular night of the invitation performance, everyone was admiring the film, supposedly safe from fire, showing on the screen when it caught alight and there was a minor conflagration; but it was not a serious fire.

I operated this camera and showed *All Hell* and was at once reprimanded and told to use a better film, the vicar was present. A first class show was given and compliments from all were received.

Haggar's first film show

THIS decided William Haggar. He would leave his theatrical career and pin his hopes in future on the cinema. He turned over his theatre to his eldest son, Will Haggar, and made himself a little portable show to go on the fairground.

The front of the show, with an outside platform, was painted to resemble Windsor Castle, and was called the Windsor Castle Biograph.

On the morning of April 5th 1898, we pushed this show on two light trolleys around to Harry Studt's fairground in Aberavon. We assembled it on our allotted site, and had a busy time erecting this wonderful cinematograph and waiting for the sun to go down because the tent was not dark enough.

The lighting in this tent or auditorium was by acetylene gas. This gas is evolved from calcium carbide and water, the generator for which was in the operating box. While the lights in the auditorium were on, the gasometer functioned very well but, when the lights were extinguished preparatory to starting the show, the damn thing kept making gas, no provision having been thought of against this contingency.

My father and brother Jim, who were operating, were in a canvas operating box with an acetylene gasometer giving off its extraneous fumes, two high powered gas cylinders, a linen bag full of inflammable films – and they escaped unhurt! Needless to say, the acetylene generator was hastily discarded in favour of the old fashioned naptha lamps which were so very successful on the fairgrounds in those days. There were eight naptha lamps on the exterior of the show and one inside; this one had to be removed when the show was about to proceed.

At the first public performance the little show was packed with about 250-300 people. Naturally my father, being the chief operator, was extremely nervous and anxious that it should go well. We had a Lecturer to describe the films, which would consist of possibly seven of the short subjects as previously enumerated, with an interval between each to fit up the next one.

Unfortunately, after a short time, so hot, so anxious was father as he bent and peered over his machine to make sure the film was threaded correctly, that the perspiration from his manly brow steamed the lenses fore and aft, and he could not get even a glimmer of light on the screen. In despair he spoke to the Lecturer: "For God's sake say something!"

The Lecturer looked at the screen and said: "Ladies and Gentlemen, if you could see this picture, it would be a train emerging from a tunnel!"

This unhappy state of affairs continued for the first two performances but by this time the heat from the projecting light had overcome the mist on the lens, and the last three performances were quite good.

We had effects for all the films, kettle drum and drum for Train *Emerging from a Tunnel* etc., and I was usually responsible for these 'noises off'.

We realised £15 from the five performances on the first day, the admission prices being three pence and two pence. I heard my father, with a gasp of satisfaction, say to my two elder brothers when he counted the cash, "I knew there was money in it."

*Rose Haggar in
the costume of
a 'Parader'.*

I shall never forget the excitement of the first opening of this cinematograph show. As stated before, we had to wait for sundown to enable us to show at all.

Our main advertisement consisted of the outside attraction of a small brass band, four instruments including myself. The bandsmen wore frock coats similar to Buster and Mimlaters' Menagerie. I had on my frock coat but I had deferred putting on my top hat until the last moment. When the call came for playing, I removed my cap for safety, putting it in the bell of one of the larger brass instruments.

This put that instrument out of action, and for sheer nervousness, inefficiency and lack of practice, I measure that brass band as second to none. But, despite this catastrophe, we drew five full houses that day.

Before going further, I think I should make it clear that the writings in this book apply to South Wales only; I have no idea whatever of what might have been happening in other parts of the country.

On April 5th we showed at Aberavon Fair. It was a fine day and we collected £15 but the second day, Tuesday April 6th, we only collected 15 shillings. The public were evidently not impressed by the fiasco of our 'blackout' first attempt.

However, we were in the fairground business. We pulled down our show and moved away to Pontypridd to another branch of the Studt family. Here we made an addition to our brass band with a professional cornet player and, I must say, the band was reasonably efficient for its purpose.

Pontypridd, the centre of the Welsh coalfield, is half way up the Rhondda Valley and was well known to the fairground community as coal land and, no doubt, we should have done remarkably well there over the Easter Holiday but it rained incessantly the whole of the time. On Easter Monday 1898 we did not take one penny piece. Not a very encouraging start! We could possibly have taken £15 - £25 on that Easter Monday, so it was rather disappointing to take nothing and get wet into the bargain.

Early days of the Cinematograph Show

THIS petty misfortune was backed by a greater misfortune: a coal strike which lasted in South Wales for six months. We moved on to Ross and what is known as private business. In fairgrounds a fair is a fair but when a show is opened anywhere else, between the fairs, it is private business.

We never did so well in private business as in fairs; true to form we did not do very well in Ross. One reason for the poor business probably, was that people simply did not know what we were offering them.

Nobody had heard of a cinematograph, nobody had seen a cinematograph. In fact when we were touting and requesting them to come into the show, they wondered what we were talking about.

We moved from Ross to Hereford, where we had a site in Broad Street, which was secondary to High Town, and there we did reasonably well considering the many factors we had against us. It was here we first saw Wadbrook's huge travelling cinema. We went round once or twice and saw the people pouring in and out of their show as fast as they could take the money.

This, once again, confirmed father's conviction that there was money in it – although we didn't see much of it!

Wadbrook's was a fine show. They had recently turned to the cinematograph business from what was known as a 'Ghost Show'; they knew the business, they had the experience, they were organised, they knew how to appeal to the people and how to get them in.

We were still strange to the business of film showing, having the whole of our lives been used to a steadier pace in the theatrical business. Father was not deterred. The optimism which had stood him in good stead all of his life did not falter. We had 'burned our boats' and could not go back; we could only go forward.

We went on from Hereford to Builth Fair. This was a long journey, 40 miles by rail – and rail travel was expensive, especially to us! To our surprise at Builth Fair, we found we were doing remarkably well. On the first day we had three full shows (which by now, incidentally, were running smoothly).

We were doing so well when, lo and behold, the cinematograph machine broke down! This, of course, happened at the height of our busy time on Fair Night.

Were we dismayed? We were not.

When the original equipment was bought at Exeter, it included hundreds of lantern slides, one very fine set being 'Victoria's Glorious Reign', which dealt with the life and reign of her late Majesty. There was a printed descriptive lecture to accompany these slides.

Well, it was Fair Night, the people were there, and they wanted to come into the show. Nobody knew what a cinematograph was – at least very few did – so we touted the abridged version of 'Victoria's Glorious Reign' and everyone, except one old gentleman, was very pleased. The aforementioned old gentleman had seen a cinematograph show before!

We repeated this performance two, if not three times the same evening until the close of the fair that night.

Meanwhile the cinematograph had to be repaired. Father found that it would have to be taken to London so he took it up the next day; travelling expenses were four pounds and the cost of the repair sixpence. One tiny screw had shaken out which anyone with a screwdriver could have replaced had they been able to find it!

WE went from Builth Fair to Welsh Hay where there was another fair, but here we came up against some opposition – we found another cinematograph show on the same ground.

This belonged to Bill Samuels of Swansea, the one time celebrated Welsh pugilist who did a very fine boxing show and a small cinematograph show, and was very jealous of our intrusion in what might be called his own domain.

Bill Samuels (God rest his soul; a good man in his own line) used to refer to father as 'the old mummer', obviously referring to his play acting days (play acting being known as mumming and the shows being called mumming booths).

On this occasion we were standing next to Mr Samuels' Boxing Show and, when opening time came for us the night before the fair at 7 o'clock, we turned out our little brass band to play some music to attract the crowd but Mr Samuels thought differently. Every time we turned out our band, Bill Samuels turned out his boxers, their raucous voices touting their own show.

This rather took the wind out of our sails: we could not get the people round to what we had to offer and in the end we retired into our show in ignominy. But Father's persistence would not be suppressed.

"Time to organise things," he said to our cornet player; "You have been in the army, haven't you?"

"Yes, Governor."

"When I say Go! You go out and blow bugle calls towards Bill Samuels' show until I tell you to stop."

Another man was told to bang the big drum until told to stop. Father was directing the battle: he waited until Mr. Samuels had finished springing his lines and had a nice crowd of people round him listening to what he had to say, and then he gave the word. With drum and bugle we surged forth and would not desist.

'Bang, Bang, Bang' we repeated until poor Mr. Samuels was almost demented; he turned towards father saying: "Stop that ruddy drum!"

We did not stop and Bill Samuels and his boxers took their turn to retire into their show in ignominy.

The crowds were enjoying this rivalry. And Father, ever ready to seize an opportunity, invited the public into his show free. We had a packed house and it proved to be an excellent advertisement; we did very well on the two following days.

THE first mechanism of a Triunial Lantern was made by John Wrench of 50 Gray's Inn Road, London. It had a sprocket and no locking ring, and the mechanism was similar to the free wheel of a bicycle. There were a series of cocks which were pushed one by one the necessary distance in the necessary direction.

The shutter, by the way, was a rear barrel shutter, which strange to say, after the elapse of over fifty years has been resuscitated and insisted upon by the authorities today. Also I should like to say that the outfit bought in Exeter for £80 included six gas cylinders of 100 cubic feet capacity, each enclosed in substantial coconut matting sacks for safety. Two of these cylinders were intended to be in use, two in reserve, and two in transit to and from Brent's Oxygen Company, Birmingham, where the empty cylinders had to be returned for refilling.

Also included in our equipment were sets of lenses both for the biunial lanterns and for the cinematograph, for adjusting the size of the picture to the length of the throw. There were also hundreds of lantern slides.

As for films, we never seemed to stop buying them until the film companies modernised their methods and initiated a hiring and sharing system. In fact, in the later years we were paying at the rate of £1,000 per year for buying films. Unfortunately this collection of films, which would have been of inestimable value today, were destroyed carelessly and deliberately just to get rid of them, although it was partly due to the fact that they were a source of danger from fire.

One tea chest of films was sold to a dealer in 1924 for £5 and, when he came to examine them, he found that he was buying back some of the films he had supplied to us twenty years earlier. Their ultimate destination I do not know.

Wrench Model ''C' projector c1905 – part of an early silent 35mm projector believed to have been owned and used by William Haggar.
National Library Wales

Hard times and the one penny show

FROM Welsh Hay Fair in 1898 we took courage and went back to Mountain Ash in South Wales, after being persuaded to do so by that stout old trooper Harry Studt Senior.

The Welsh strike had been on then for six weeks: Mountain Ash Fair came on Whit Sunday and we attended. Father spoke to the crowds:

"Ladies and Gentlemen, we are amongst you once more and on consultation with my worthy friend, Harry Studt, we do not see fit that you should be deprived of your annual fair although you have been on strike a considerable time. We know you have not much money, so to enable you to see what we have to offer in the way of entertainment, we have decided to show for the humble sum of one penny."

He intended to say a lot more but he had no time. The people crowded in at every available entrance with their pennies in their hands and we were busy all day taking more money, at one penny a time, than we had taken all the previous month!

One old lady, who seemed impressed by the frock coats and top hats of our little brass band, asked us whether we were in mourning! Very soon after this, Father, feeling that something must be done to create a better impression, exchanged the somewhat funereal uniform for some second hand Cherry Pickers' uniforms with brass buttons, gold braid and peaked caps. This effect, when backed by the Windsor Castle front of the show, inspired another old lady: "I was in your barracks last night!"

Our well-tried motto of 'stick to the coal' was exemplified at Mountain Ash but unfortunately, after visiting Treorchy Fair and Builth, we left Wales again. We went to Chepstow and Lydney and the result was near starvation.

This state of affairs prevailed for all the summer months of 1898. We were reduced to dispensing with our two living wagons, proceeding as best we could with the two trailers; we slept where we could and ate when we could afford it.

That was a bad time. People did not know what a cinematograph was; they did not know what we were offering them and we seemed unable to convince them. The agricultural areas of Wiltshire and Gloucester did not receive us with open arms and the Welsh strike was still proceeding.

IT WAS after these hard summer months that we thankfully heard of the termination of the strike. We returned to Wales to a place called Cwmbran, where we did not have very much business.

Then Father decided on a tour of the halls in South Wales with the pantomime *Cinderella*, thus risking the loss of all his remaining financial resources. It was a lucky gamble, however, and the tour was an immense financial success.

There had been no entertainment of this kind in South Wales during the whole of the six unfortunate months of the coal strike and it seemed that we were first in everywhere and could not go wrong.

The 'Chrono' – the King of Bioscopes.

We showed seven days a week at three towns a week, a pantomime on weekdays and what was billed as a 'Sacred Concert' on Sundays. This Sunday concert was a very fine show which began with an opening hymn; then, with the use of the biunial lantern and biograph, we illustrated various songs such as *Star of Bethlehem* and fine dramatic recitations, finishing with a Passion Play on the biograph and another hymn.

We were packed to suffocation for these Sacred Concerts, and received great commendations everywhere we went.

The tour included Pembrokeshire, which was virgin ground as far as we were concerned, and it was on this tour that we personally contacted the Pembrokeshire Imperial Yeomanry, who invariably occupied the best seats wherever we went.

Some of the towns included on this tour were Haverfordwest, Milford Haven, Pembroke, Pembroke Dock, Carmarthen, Fishguard etc., and this part of the country was to stand us in good stead for many years to come, as we had the honour of standing in Pembroke Town itself for the annual October Fair for nineteen years in succession, and did remarkably good business on every visit.

The theatrical tour ended where it had begun, at Cwmbran, my father being anxious to get back on the road with his little cinematograph show once more. He was still convinced that there was money in it.

We made a new show-front comprising two living wagons. My elder brother went off again on his own, while we made a return visit to Aberavon. It was at the time of the April Fair, and we did very good business.

We were by now more experienced in the ways and means of getting people to part with their coppers to see our show. We discarded the triunial lantern and the Wrench machine in favour of Messrs. Maguire & Baucus' Bioscope. The London manager of this firm was the celebrated Charles Urban.

This bioscope had a cam movement; it struck the films down and swivelled towards the operator for re-threading, bringing the lantern lens in focus using one light only. By that time there were spools to hold a thousand feet or more, and take-up to accept the unwinding film; these stood us in good stead for many years.

We visited Aberdare April Fair for the first time then, not allowing ourselves to be guided by our previous experience, we left Wales again confident that we would do well this time. We ran in the same counties as before but, alas, our hopes were not realised; we had another bad year.

In August at Gloucester the show, comprising four vans, was actually on the railway trucks, and father was wondering which way to go. His great friend of the fairgrounds in this part of the country, William Symonds, was doing his best to persuade father to take the show to the Trowbridge Flower Show and my brother Jim was persuading him very strongly to go back to Wales. Father was between the devil and the deep blue sea, but common sense and financial difficulties urged him to return to Wales. We went to Wales (it was then August 1899) and we pitched at Ebbw Vale Market Place; from then on we 'stuck to the coal' and could not go wrong.

We were under the impression that a travelling cinematograph show was not a good proposition in the winter months, so we laid up this show at Mountain Ash and again went out on tour with the theatre.

This time Father and Jim went into partnership and the show was known as W & J Haggar's Dramatic Company. We went to Pembrokeshire and presented the play *The Penalty of Crime,* including a bioscope display and the inevitable Sunday concert – and, I may say, that in most places it was the Sunday concert that paid the rent.

Improving technology

THE WINTER tour finished at Brynamman on the 1st March 1900 and we again went back to our travelling cinematograph show, which opened at Aberdare in April with a new double wagon front.

We were, incidentally, still using limelight. It was during this period that Charles Urban brought out a new kind of bioscope with no shutter, although it still had a cam movement. The idea was that, if the movement was quick enough, no shutter was necessary.

We endured this new system for possibly six months when Charles Urban achieved something better. It was the addition of an expanding shutter – his argument then being that a shutter improved the picture if it was small enough – so he devised a shutter which would increase or decrease as necessary.

It was also around this time (I cannot be quite sure when)

that Robert W. Paul & Co. launched a very fine cinematograph with a pin-operated intermittent sprocket wheel, but there was no locking ring.

I am afraid that this was not an unqualified success. This intermittent sprocket had a locking device, a flat spring about two inches long with a round knob on the end which was supposed to spring out and in again to hold the sprocket rigid when necessary; unfortunately, it did not stand up to its work.

During that summer Messrs. Maguire & Baucus and Charles Urban had a High Court case in London concerning the word 'Bioscope'. Charles Urban, having been employed by Messrs. Maguire & Baucus, was leaving the firm and setting up on his own. He intended using the word 'Bioscope' in his business but Maguire & Baucus claimed the word as their trade mark and sole property.

Father was an important witness in this case to prove the word 'Bioscope' was in general use. This was proved to the Court's satisfaction and Maguire and Baucus lost their case.

It was also during this summer that the introduction of the periodicity blade occurred, although it was not generally accepted.

Father went to Charles Urban and asked if he had heard of Paul's idea of a double shutter. "Don't think much of it," said Charles Urban, so Father told him to send out for a sheet of violet gelatine. This was done.

Father asked if there was a film he could use. They went into the show room and the film was shown with the one-blad-ed shutter. It was re-wound and shown with the double-bladed shutter which father had made from the sheet of violet gelatine. Charles Urban was delighted and, chewing his inevitable cigar, he said: "We will adopt it Daddy."

This type of shutter is in universal use today. On some occasions Pathé put out a machine with a three-bladed shutter and all types and sizes of double and triple-bladed shutters were experimented with, but the two-bladed shutter, as demonstrated on that day to Charles Urban, retains its position universally today.

WE continued on our way and our tour of South Wales included Pembrokeshire for the summer months, then back to Aberavon, Neath and Llanelli Fairs for the autumn.

Since then, we were fortunate to have Aberdare Market Place as a winter headquarters each year. We were not the only show travelling Wales at that time, and our main opposition was Wadbrook's under the able management of Harry Scard Senior, who was in control of a very fine electrically lit parading front show which took the cream of the money everywhere.

It was during the winter of 1901 that Mr Scard surprised everybody by having the Welsh international football matches at Cardiff filmed and showing them exclusively in his own show. This was quite a walkover for Wadbrook's! Good luck to them! During our tour of Pembrokeshire, while at Pembroke Dock, Father had sent out an order for a portable electric generating engine costing £600.

We had had enough of the eccentricities of limelight and decided that electricity was necessary for our business; the money was paid while the going was good.

At the beginning of the year 1901 we were still on limelight. We continued our tour from Aberdare and eventually returned to Treorchy Fair; this was a very important time for us because our new portable engine and generating set was to arrive there. It was a heavy, cumbersome affair and gave us a great deal of trouble by sinking in the fields – and for the next four or five years whilst touring south Wales we were always in trouble whenever the fairgrounds were soft or muddy. We were never free from anxiety with this infernal portable engine; nevertheless it was a master of its work when in 'situ'.

Needless to say, it added greatly to the appearance of the front of the show and seemed to attract more people than ever: it certainly improved the showing of the films as, although limelight had stood us in good stead up till then, it was not nearly as good as electric light.

I think it was the effect of this electric light and engine that induced us to spend the winters as well as the summers with this show instead of going back into the theatrical business.

It was at this same Treorchy Fair, on the first Saturday after Whit Sunday 1902, that we found a rival cinema show – that of the celebrated Richard Dooner from Devonshire. He had decided to make South Wales his happy hunting ground.

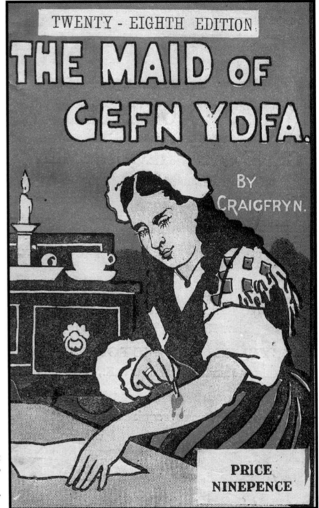

The tale of 'The Maid of Cefn Ydfa' inspired the Haggars' first scripted film.

Chapter 4
William Haggar Turns Film-maker by Walter Haggar

IT WAS not long after Wadbrooks's filming the international football matches that Father decided to buy a cinematograph camera of his own, and in June of the following year we bought a camera with tripod and a roll of film – 350 feet – which in those days was one shilling a foot.

We were then at Burry Port, near Llanelli. Well, we had the camera and it was not long before we were looking for something to film; what could we take? We decided to go round to the station, and there took a film of *A Train Entering Burry Port Station*.

That was our first filming effort, the first of many great successes and a few failures. With added zest we took many topical items, including football matches which were very popular. Eventually we acted small plays, one our most successful being *A Phantom Ride through Swansea* which was filmed from the front of a tram.

During the following year, my brother Will was showing his theatre at Maesteg. The weather was fine (the weather being a deciding factor in the taking of films in those days), so we took the train to Maesteg where we induced Will's theatrical company to act something for us to film. What film should we take? we wondered. We had no scenery and there was not much time for rehearsal. Will wanted to put on *The Dumb Man of Manchester* but eventually I insisted on the taking of a Welsh local story entitled *The Maid of Cefn Ydfa*.

We shot that film in an hour and a half, there being seven scenes, and the total length of the film being approximately 450 feet. This film was to bring in hundreds and hundreds of pounds. It was dispatched to the photographers and returned to Treorchy by the following Wednesday when, at the admission price of two pence and three pence, we took forty pounds – and for years after, this film did similar business throughout the whole of South Wales and was the despair of our rival shows.

We had this film re-taken years later at Pontardulais by a cameraman employed from London, the total length of the film this time being 3,000 feet. This edition too was a very great success.

THE following winter I was on the lookout for improvements, and changed from the Urban bioscope to the Pathé No. 2 machine.

The Urban bioscope still had a cam movement, but Pathé's had the Maltese cross and the locking ring on the intermittent sprocket, which was a decided improvement.

But, alas, there were only two sprocket wheels, the feed was at the top of the intermittent and there was no take-up. The film ran loose below the stand and was wound up by hand by a lad seated on a stool. Despite these liabilities the results of the projection from the Pathé machine were so good that we adopted this method and it stood us in good stead for many years.

We had our own lantern made to accommodate the Pathé mechanism, the lantern incorporating two arc lamps, the one for the Pathé mechanism and the other for the lantern slides.

At this stage we were bothered by insufficient current in the arc lamps but a very good friend of ours, Mr. Tetlow, who was in charge of the cinematograph department of Moss Empires Ltd., instructed us how to wire up the lamp, i.e. five circuits on to one pair of carbons, and we could get all the light we wanted.

Three years later in 1905, I myself instructed Mr. Tilney how to wire up his arc lamp in a new cinema he was building. It was during the First World War that Mr. Tilney built the Capitol in Cardiff. In those days he set the pace for modern cinemas in the area.

As a matter of interest, I remember that his particular advertising poster showed a finger pointing and the wording, 'Capitol Cardiff – a thousand seats and one for YOU'

EACH summer when the weather was fine (especially when in Pembrokeshire) we would take our own films. It was probably in the year 1903 when we returned to Maesteg and one afternoon we set out with some dogs, a coconut shy net, a live rabbit, a camera and the actors from my brother's portable theatre – as usual with no script.

Asking no one's permission we went up into the hills, arranged, rehearsed and took a film called *The Poachers*. Did you ever see a rabbit caught in a coconut shy net?

This film was a huge success. I must try and make it clear that when we took these films we retained the sole rights of showing in South Wales and anything good was marketed.

This particular film *The Poachers* sold no less than 470 copies in one year, being marketed by Gaumont. In fact the success of this film prompted the remark by Charles Urban: "You should not help these little firms Daddy!" – this being addressed to my father.

Gaumont in those days was controlled by A.C. and R.C. Bromhead, two brothers and very close friends of my father. In fact they considered our camera work so good that a little later on they presented us with an up-to-date cinematograph camera and a very fine tripod with a mechanical revolving head, all gratis!

They also gave us one of their latest projecting mechanisms of the cam type, but this we could not accept, the reason being that the cam struck the film on the emulsion side and we were afraid – in fact we were sure – it would damage our valuable collection of films. So we graciously declined this handsome gift with thanks.

Father was an expert photographer. For instance, when we took films, he always snipped off four to six inches of the film and developed it himself, taking cognizance of the quality and exposure etc., always trying to improve his work.

At this time we had a very fine half-plate camera and two quarter-plate snapshot cameras, and at every available opportunity we were taking either films or snapshots of local scenes, events and personalities. For instance on the day following the erection of our portable cinema, father would take his snapshot camera, charged with a dozen quarter plates, and wander round the town seeking local colour – old ladies, children, groups of boys, anything of interest.

Still from 'A Desperate Poaching Affray'.

On returning home he would develop the plates himself, make lantern slides of the Bromide type and they were washed, dried and on the screen the same night. This was an advantage not shared by any of the other touring cinema shows.

Many amusing incidents occurred over this snapshot-cum-slide part of the entertainment. If Father saw an interesting old lady, he would say, "just a minute, Ma" and a close-up photograph of her would appear on our screen the same night.

We have had requests from relatives: "Please Mr. Haggar, don't put Mother on the show tonight."

In Milford Haven, in the Fish Market, it did not take the fishermen and boys long to get to know father's intentions as regards these snaps; in fact he had a job to get away from them. This of course, was just a side-line and didn't form the main part of the entertainment but it was an agreeable adjunct.

William Haggar caught on camera in 'The Stepney Wedding'
– a rare film appearance.

I believe the hand camera used for these snaps was supplied by Messrs. Cricks & Martin who gave us some very valuable advice. They pointed out where the cinema was going and tried to induce father to abandon the showing of films and concentrate on the taking of them, but we could not see the drift of things then.

The same advice was given us in a more definite form by a well known personage, Leon Vint of Abertillary, in the spring of 1908 or thereabouts. "Haggar," he said, "you're on the wrong track – all this labour and moving the show from place to place; why don't you get a series of halls for continuous showing? It will be all the rage. I have already got Neath (and several others were mentioned). You, with your boys, should establish a circuit at once while you have the opportunity, and while the going is good."

Traction Engines and elaborate show-fronts

BUT ONCE more we could not see eye-to-eye – and once more I am ahead of my story. I was stressing the turmoil of getting this show about by rail – horses being too much of a burden.

Eventually we decided to go in for a traction engine. We invested in this engine in about 1904/5 and it was delivered in March to Brynmawr, the heavy portable engine going to light my brother Will's portable theatre at New Tredegar.

I remember an interview between Mr. Robinson, traveller to John Fowler and Co. of Leeds, when, after stating the particulars of the traction engine and telling us of its virtues, Father asked him: "Do I get anything off if I pay cash?"

"Can you pay cash?"

Violet Haggar in Boer War costume. The war was the subject of several films.

"Do I get anything off if I pay cash?"

"Why, yes," was the answer. "You get ten percent and two and a half percent."

"That makes twelve and a half percent," said father.

"No," said Mr Robinson. "Ten percent first and two and a half percent for the balance."

"Do it up," said father, "I will pay cash."

He learned that he would save £90. Mr. Robinson closed his book, looked over his glasses and said: "You are the only showman who has ever paid cash for an engine."

When our traction engine arrived it had fine nameplates which stated that it was christened the 'Maid of Cefn Ydfa' and had a brass nameplate on the back:

Bought for cash...The 'Maid of Cefn Ydfa'.

'Owners: W. Haggar and Sons, South Wales'. This nameplate caused a mild sensation among other showmen because the majority of their engines had the owner's nameplate hidden in some inaccessible corner. We still have this nameplate: at present it adorns the front door of Mr. Leonard Haggar's Cinema, Main Street, Pembroke, of which he is the owner.

This traction engine was a fine machine and eased the work of transport immensely. Instead of paying rail charges and horse hire, we just purchased half a ton of coal and we were able to cover a larger field of operations.

One step leads to another and our little home-made show-fronts were getting rather out of date, and we were wondering how we could improve things further – never forgetting for one moment that the most important part of the entertainment was inside the show. A clean screen, a good light and good pictures were always our first consideration.

I call to mind one visit to Treorchy: there were seven cinematographs in a circle. All were electrically lit and had attractive show-fronts, parading girls and jugglers to attract the crowds. They did attract the crowds - so did we!

But they attracted the crowds for one or two nights; we attracted them every night. Why? We always had a change of programme and always found time on the busiest fair day (when we might do 15 to 20 performances) to show on the screen the forthcoming attractions.

Where we were able to give a fresh programme every day for a fortnight, the other shows had very few films, and could only show the same ones night after night, relying more on their outside attractions to draw the crowds.

Included in this circle of shows were Chipperfield's Circus and Pictures, Cedric's Menagerie and Pictures, Wadbrook's, Dooners, Relph and Pedley's, Anderton's & Rowland's and Haggar's, and I must say there was enough entertainment on the exterior of these shows in this circle without anybody paying a penny to go inside; it was a very fine fair, no doubt.

However, we still wanted a new show-front, and were contemplating whether we should buy a double wagon carved and gilded front which at the time was being offered for sale by Orton & Co. of Burton on Trent, when one evening at tea-time, with no appointment, in walked Jim Wentworth agent for Charles Marenghi & Co., Organ Builders of Paris.

He brought with him a large scale drawing of a very fine 44ft. organ and show-front combined with a double entrance (all travelling shows in those days had one central entrance: the engine generating the electric light would be on one side and the old barrel organ on the left).

This organ was such a great step forward from the general run of organs: we were just a little dubious as to its ability to maintain what they claimed for it. But it was a very fine piece of work and Jim Wentworth received an order within an hour on the proviso that his firm kept the organ in tune for twelve months. This request was gladly granted.

They promised to keep it in tune for one year and deliver it by the following April (in the spring of 1906); in one leap we went right to the top in the cinematograph business.

THE organ and show-front with its workmanship and gilded figures was a marvellous piece of work. It could play paper music, songs, overtures, anything you wanted – and the crowds used to stand enthralled with its grandeur.

Incorporated in the front were 840 incandescent lamps of various colours. Each lamp had to be in its own particular place – the gold leaf of a flower would warrant an amber lamp, a spray of violets a curving of violet lamps, red costumes on the paintings called for red lamps and so on.

There were three separate electrical circuits embracing the whole of the front of this organ. When these three circuits were illuminated simultaneously, the whole of this 44 ft. organ resembled a large church window. No wonder the crowds stayed for hours to watch this display, it was wonderful.

These circuits worked mechanically but were not timed to the music so we worked these by hand keeping in time with the various tempos as the music was playing. The two favourite tunes for this operation were *The Village Blacksmith* and *The Halleluiah Chorus*. Needless to say all the main lighting was extinguished whilst this display was in progress.

We were now firmly established and all the other travelling cinema shows were forced to follow suit and alter their fronts, making them all double entranced and there were, in the course of a year or eighteen months, some very fine adaptations and alterations – keeping in line with 'the old man'.

More film making

I HAVE not yet mentioned that we took our own films of the Boer War, and these were very successful. There was a firm in Blackburn which turned out some very fine Boer War films (this was, of course, much earlier than the period of our new organ show-front, being in 1899 - 1902) and we followed their example, taking most of them on the Welsh hills of the Rhondda Valley.

We also took some Russo-Japanese War films on the snow-clad tops of the hills above the Rhymney Valley but this was, of course, a few years later.

In the spring of 1903 we were at Port Talbot and, on a very fine windy Sunday, Mumbles Lifeboat set out from Mumbles (goodness knows why, there had been no call out), sailed across Swansea Bay, lost its rudder and was dashed to pieces on the breakwater of Aberavon Docks in view of hundreds of people.

Six men were drowned and the onlookers could only watch helplessly. There was a mass funeral at Mumbles the following week and we decided to film this. We took the camera down to Port Talbot station to proceed to Swansea en route to Mumbles and who was at the station but Harry Scard Senior, who was also the possessor of a cinematograph camera.

Unfortunately for him, his camera was at Maesteg where his show was situated at the time. He had overlooked this event and was extremely cross about it. He came up to father and, upon learning where we were going and what we contemplated doing, he exclaimed, "Ought to be horse-whipped. I ought to be horse-whipped!"

Then he said, "Well if you get anything, can I have a copy of the film?"

"Certainly," he was told.

Mr. Scard got his copy and did remarkably good business with it – as also did Moss Empires, Cardiff, Newport and Swansea!

Another incident of early film making took place at Quaker's Yard in 1904/5 where we were taking a Russo-Japanese War film. I myself acted the part of a little Jap, and my brother James (a burly fellow) was a Russian. The film was arranged, staged and fought with bayonets and guns and it was decided that, at the conclusion of the fight, the Jap should stab the Russian.

Haggar's Royal Bioscope 1906. The show front was lit by 840 incandescent, multi-coloured light bulbs. A magnificent 44ft. long, 94 key Marenghi organ stood in all its grandeur at mid-stage position and there were at least seven carved statues covered in gold leaf. Electricity was provided by the traction engine 'The Maid of Cefn Ydfa'.

William Haggar filming at Tenby Fair in 1906.

When the camera stopped, the burly Russian put his hand to his head and withdrew it covered in blood! In the excitement of the film I had stabbed him in reality, and he was bleeding profusely. In fact, in most of the melées of film making, there were wounds, cuts and bruises but they were never noticed until later.

By now we had established a good reputation for taking films, and on one occasion were requested by Mr. Richard Dooner, who also had a cine camera, to take a film of a walking match at Treorchy.

An assistant and myself set off in the pony and trap and secured a pretty good film of this walking match for Mr. Dooner. It was, of course, a topical film and purely of local interest, but stood him in good stead up and down the Rhondda Valley for a time.

A year or two later we received some assistance and co-operation from Moss Empires, Cardiff, in taking a film of the Welsh National Pageant there. A copy of this film is today in the Welsh National Museum, Cardiff, in a sealed metal container.

Experiments with sound and colour

FATHER died before the advent of talking films. Although we had experimented and made every effort to incorporate sight with sound, the nearest we ever got was with an instrument called the Cinephone, marketed, I believe, by Haydon and Urry and the Walturdaw Firm.

This comprised a gramophone with a turntable, to which was attached an illuminated disc and four illuminated dots at each quarter of a revolving finger. On the left hand bottom corner of the film being shown was a replica of this revolving finger and the four dots, and it was the operator's duty to keep these two revolving fingers in similar positions by passing the dots at the same moment (most cinemas in those days being turned by hand).

If the operator could keep these two revolving fingers at corresponding positions, sight and sound were in synchronisation, but this was an extremely difficult task and not very successful. In any case, it was only the short songs that we attempted such as *Oh! Oh! Antonio* and *The Shade of the old Apple Tree*.

Another very fine apparatus for the incorporation of sound was the Auxetophone, marketed by The Gramophone & Typewriter Company. This machine had a special sound box on the Aeolian Harp principle, and constituted air under four points of pressure being forced through a grid in the sound box, which gave a very pure and powerful tone to any gramophone record.

This instrument cost about £111 but it was well worth it, although it was merely used for playing choice gramophone records illuminated by lantern slides. These were the two major attempts at incorporating sight and sound until the eventual start of talking films.

I MUST mention in passing that the Charles Urban mechanism before mentioned was on a swivel base, and pulling it in a clockwise direction towards the operator brought the slide lens in line with the arc lamp, thus enabling the screen to be occupied with either advertisements or local snaps while the operator was threading up his mechanism with the next spool.

It was some time before spool boxes became universally used: in fact, we ran for years with an open 14 inch spool at the top and bottom. In the days of the travelling cinema, a 14 inch spool would hold the whole of a programme as, with the travelling cinema show, it was not unusual to have 15 or 20 performances (or exhibitions) on a fair day, at an average time of 20 minutes each, made up of five subjects and always finishing with a comedy.

A sample programme of films would be:

1. *The Last Cartridge*.
2. *Phantom Ride through Swansea High Street*.
3. (Exciting drama): *The Poachers*.
4. (Interesting subject): *Loie Fuller in her Serpentine Dance*.
5. (The comedy): *Weary Willie and Tired Tim at the Races*.

After the show: "Side doors out, kindly recommend the entertainment to your friends."

The organ would strike up outside and we would proceed to entice and usher in another house, at admission prices of two pence and three pence.

Even at these absurdly low prices (no entertainment tax) takings on a fair day might work out at anything between forty pounds and seventy pounds all in silver, copper or a sprinkling of gold. It often happened that we were in such a hurry to reach the next town that these takings were just thrown under the bed in one of the living vans and counted at our leisure – our motto being 'get it and count it when you can'.

Father's one idea was to build up his two accounts in the bank – his current account and the surplus in his deposit account (two and a half percent undeclared). As he used to say, "If I live long enough, I shall be an old man one day and nobody wants an old man if he hasn't any money."

A FEW other firms' names come to mind as well as Charles Urban; they are Haydon and Urry, Walturdaw (which is a combination of Walker, Turner and Dawson), and Cricks and Martin, Elgé (being Gaumont), Robert W. Paul, Cecil Hepworth & Co., John Wrench & Co., and Pathé Fréres: these are some of the firms I remember with which we used to do business.

Of course in those days there were colour films very like those of today, but they were only short subjects such as *A Lady Dancing* or *A Little Tram*.

One of the biggest and best efforts at coloured film was made by George Meliés of Paris, 1,000 feet in length, entitled *Wonders of the Deep*. This cost us seventy pounds and one shilling for postage.

Father made no bones about paying seventy pounds for the film, but was quite grieved to have to pay a shilling for the postage. This film is, I believe still at our Pembroke cinema.

These films were all coloured by hand, with very fine brushes. It was a very tedious job, but the workmanship was excellent, and how on earth they managed to maintain the regular density of the colours necessary for any cinematograph film, I cannot imagine.

We ourselves once made an attempt at a colour film. We selected a short subject of a lady disrobing: her first petticoat we endeavoured to colour red and her second petticoat we tried to colour blue but, when we showed this film privately, both colours were simply alive by virtue of the varying density of the dyes employed for colouring.

Needless to say the film was shown once only and was greeted with great roars of laughter on the unfortunate occasion.

William Haggar and sons advertise their bioscope camera.
Picture: National Sound and Film Archive

The Electric Haggar's Coliseum Bioscope of 1907. Bioscope front with Gavioli Organ showing the celebrated 'Paraders' who danced on the front in their daring knee-length dresses to attract the crowds. The front of the Coliseum was a mass of gilded carvings set around the 110 key Gavioli Organ. Two of the gold leaf covered statues from the forefront of the Coliseum, known as the 'Teak Ladies', stood in floodlit alcoves in the auditorium of Haggars Cinema, Pembroke until its closure.

Chapter 5
William Haggar's First Permanent Cinemas

I WISH I could have known my great grandfather William Haggar but, of course, he died long before I was born. I am full of admiration for William and my great grandmother Sarah and wonder how on earth they managed to bring up such a large family on the road – a way of life which often meant considerable hardship.

They certainly had their fair share of grief: three of their children died young and, in September 1909, tragedy struck again when Sarah passed away. It was a huge blow and, although William continued to tour that season, he decided to forsake the travelling life and settle permanently in Aberdare which, for many years, he had made his winter base.

Its travelling days over, the Bioscope came to rest in the Market Square and was transformed into the Shanty Cinema. William resided in the living wagons behind the show with his youngest son, Henry and his daughters, Violet and Lily.

This is remembered in Aberdare: a plaque has been placed on the wall of the market place bearing the words

Arthur William Haggar (1851-1925)
Pioneer Silent Film Maker
ran his travelling cinema on this site in Market Square
c1900-1914

It was a time of change; permanent cinemas were replacing the travelling shows, and William Haggar began building up a chain of permanent cinemas. In 1910 he bought the Royalty Theatre in Llanelli which was managed by his son Jim and combined film shows with live theatre and variety.

Most showmen were adept at producing some effect to improve business, and there is a family story about Jim buying a monkey, thinking that this gimmick would help to draw the crowds. The monkey was dressed in top hat and tails and placed in the cinema foyer to entertain the public.

What Jim hadn't banked on was that the monkey had a nicotine habit and was getting through up to fifty fags a day, The takings were sadly depleted and it was not long before that monkey went up in smoke!

The Royalty was followed by the purchase of the Skating Rink at Pontardulais, which was converted into a theatre and cinema while new cinemas were built at Mountain Ash and Merthyr.

Both of William's daughters were to marry in 1912; Violet in January and Lily in August. It was the year of weddings and in March 1912 William married for the second time. May Davies was the daughter of the owner of 'The Bird in Hand', Monk Street in Aberdare.

William and May left after their wedding for London hoping to book a passage on the *Titanic*, destined for New York; it was only due to their failure to secure tickets that they escaped the tragedy. Having found a berth on another ship, they were able to spend their honeymoon in their chosen destination, New York.

Having escaped one disaster, William was to face another ordeal in New York. The couple were happily out walking one day when William suffered a stroke and lost his sight. As fortune had it, the gentleman, who came to offer assistance, was a fellow freemason from Neath! As a consequence, William received appropriate treatment and fortunately his sight returned.

On their return from New York, William deserted his living wagon for a town house in Aberdare which became known as Kinema House.

He built his own luxury permanent cinema with a seating capacity for 900 on the site of the old Drill Hall, named it the

The memorial plaque to William Haggar, Aberdare market place.

Kosy Kinema and had its name displayed in big cut-out letters down each side of the building. It was described as being the 'prettiest and best-equipped hall in South Wales'.

It was opened with great ceremony, as reported in *The Aberdare Leader* on 28th August 1915 with the headline: 'Haggar's Kosy Kinema opened by the High Constable'.

Kinema House in Aberdare; William Haggar with his wife May.

On Monday evening Councillor Haggar's New Picture Theatre in Market Street, Aberdare was opened by the High Constable Mr. Chas. Kenshole.

There was a tremendous crowd present when the High Constable, accompanied by his lady, was presented by Mr. Gwilym Davies (Messrs. John Morgan & Son Ltd.) with the opening key. Mr Kenshole just spoke a few words declaring the place open and Mr. Gwilym Davies then presented Mrs Kenshole with a handsome shower bouquet of malmaison carnations and asparagus fern with smilax; the lady bowed her acknowledgements.

Invitation cards had been sent to the ladies and gentlemen of the town and a representative company stood up to sing 'God Save the King' accompanied by Mr. Carroll's orchestra.

The High Constable then rose and addressed the audience. He said that this was the first occasion that he had been called upon to open a theatre. He, however, felt justified on that occasion in coming forward to open Mr Haggar's beautiful place of amusement for several reasons.

Mr Haggar had resided in Aberdare for many years and had associated himself with everything that was for the welfare of the town and especially had he come forward in the cause of charity. He (the speaker) felt it was his duty to come forward and give what support he possibly could. Mr Haggar had provided a building worthy of the town which, they would agree with him, had not been too fortunate in that respect.

When they looked round they found that they had everything desirable in the way of comfort. He felt sure that whatever Mr Haggar put on the screen there would be nothing objectionable, and everything to meet the most fastidious tastes. He ventured to hope that this venture of Mr Haggar's would prove a success and that he would be spared for many

William Haggar's Kosy Kinema.

years to cater for the amusement and education of the people of Aberdare. (Cheers).

Mr Louis S. Clarke, Aberdare Cinema, also addressed the audience. He said that he felt greatly honoured that he should have been selected to say a few words. It was quite delightful to know that Aberdare could boast of such a fine and luxurious place of amusement.

There could be no doubt that when such an elaborate place was erected 'Pictures' had come to stay. He was very proud to say that Mr Haggar and he were the best of friends; Mr Haggar, in fact, had been quite a father to him.

He felt that if he had not known Mr Haggar it was probable that his own cinema would not have been the success it was. He hoped that they would all patronise both places after Mr Haggar had given them such a palatial building, the Kosy Kinema.

Aberdare Market Hall.

WILLIAM was very well-liked and respected in Aberdare and did much to help the town. Takings from many of his shows were donated to charity and, during World War One, he also helped the War effort by running benefit concerts in aid of The Prince of Wales National Fund.

He became a Poor Law Guardian for the Merthyr Board and was voted in as a member of the Aberdare District Council. He was well-known for his generosity and contributed a considerable sum towards the building of a new wing for the Aberdare Hospital.

By the end of the War, William was not as active as he had been and had slowed down considerably. He was heartbroken when his second wife May died in August 1924 at the early age of forty and he passed away soon afterwards on 4th February, 1925 at his son Walter's house 'Maes-yr-haf', Elm Grove, Aberdare at the age of 73.

A memorial to William Haggar stands in Aberdare cemetery.

A letter published in *The Aberdare Leader* in 1925, following William's death, shows just how well he was thought of:

Mr Editor,- *There has just 'passed on' a very familiar and beloved personality whom some called 'Old Haggar' and some who were more familiar with him in later and more private life called 'Dear Old Willie Haggar'. Both were terms of endearment; he loved all and was beloved by all.*

As we say he has 'passed on', but has he not left to many of us of this generation food for thought? And if we do but think, we shall see that he has – unconsciously perhaps – left us some lessons that we may lay to heart.

Perhaps one is most important and it is this: that he who is upright in all his dealings and who endeavours to bear the burden of the day – however heavy that burden may be – must succeed in life.

Mr. Haggar's life commenced in very humble circumstances, and it is always delightful to hear of his reminiscences, and to gather therefrom the cheery manner in which he must have faced and overcome hardships such as are not often encountered by many in these days. The experience of those days of trial toughened an already strong 'will to attain', and he did attain and to a good purpose.

Mr. Haggar in his experience encountered many vicissitudes, and whilst he was meeting them and overcoming them he became imbued with a great love of his fellows, and a longing to be of help to those not so able as he was to overcome the difficulties of the strenuous life he and they were leading.

William Haggar's generosity inspired this Christmas card, illustrated in the cinema trade paper, 'The Bioscope'.

Many have lived and still live to thank and bless the hand that was held forth to help them. The dear departed sought competence not for its own sake, but rather for the good it enabled him to do.

He was generous, not merely in the meaning of the word - that of giving money (his purse was always open in a good cause) – but in the higher sense. There ever emanated from his spirit that 'something' which impelled him to do good.

And in the latter days, Mr. Editor, when he became settled amongst us, there beamed forth, apparent to all, those noble qualities with which Nature had endowed him; that glorious and lovable simplicity; that ever readiness to advise and do good to all and sundry.

And to those who knew him intimately, there are brought to mind many acts of kindness on his part that have lifted some who were in despair out of the depths into a brighter and more hopeful outlook on life.

Such very shortly were Mr. Haggar's attributes. May Mr. Haggar's family and friends be comforted in the thought that although he has 'passed on', his memory will be cherished and held in love and reverence by all.

The Kosy Kinema burned down and is now a Ladbroke's.

WILLIAM left the Kosy Kinema to his son Walter who had been managing it prior to his father's death. Walter sold it in 1927 to Captain Willis, whose family were to own many cinemas in South Wales.

The Kosy stood next to the 1914 Court House, designed by the Aberdare born architect George Emanuel Kenshole but sadly it no longer exists having been gutted by fire in 1946.

Today Ladbroke's betting shop occupies the site and, although the Court House remains, it is now a night club.

PART TWO
The Haggars in Pembroke
'Remarkably good business...'

Chapter 6
Pembroke Fair

WILLIAM Haggar's Company visited Pembroke for many years, first with his travelling theatre and then, from 1898, with his travelling cinema or Bioscope.

Walter wrote in his memoirs: "This part of the country was to stand us in good stead for many years to come, as we had the honour of standing in Pembroke Town itself for the annual October Fair for 19 years in succession, and did remarkably good business on every visit."

Haggar's Bioscope was once a star attraction at Pembroke's Michaelmas Fair and was always built up in front of the Wesleyan Chapel in St. Michael's Square.

Pembroke Fair dates back to medieval times when the right to hold markets and fairs was granted in its charters. The present day fun fair was formerly a hiring fair where bargains were struck with local farmers for a year's work and farm workers flocked to it from all over South Pembrokeshire. This large gathering in turn attracted traders and entertainers, among them William Haggar.

Although Haggar's show was a familiar sight at the fairgrounds, it did run as a stand-alone private business too, wherever a place could be found to set up the show. However, business was always better at the fairs where the many and varying lines of businesses and attractions drew large crowds.

These included the larger rides owned by the Studts and the Danters, who still uphold the tradition of the travelling fair and are still to be seen at Pembroke Fair. There would also have been other bioscopes competing for business on the fairground: notably Dooner's Bioscope, Wadbrook's Palace, Studt's Electric Pavilion, Crecraft's Show and Danter's Coliseum.

Pembroke Fair was always held on the first working day nearest to the 10th October and used to stay ten days; now it stands for only three days. It was traditionally opened by the Mayor and the Town Crier from under the old Elm Tree, which grew in the garden of Hamilton House, and there dignitaries stood whilst the fairgoers gathered around in the Square below.

Pembroke Michaelmas Fair 1907. Haggar's Bioscope would have been a major attraction.

Elm Tree Square was always the place in the town where people gathered to hear announcements and sing carols at Christmas: in years past it was the place of the stocks and, some say, the gallows!

The Fair now takes place on the second Thursday of October and is still opened to the familiar "Oyez! Oyez! Oyez!" of the Town Crier, just as it was all those years ago when Haggar's Bioscope was the main attraction.

The event begins at Pembroke Town Hall where Town Councillors accompanied by the Chairman of the Showman's Guild, presently Abe Danter, local dignitaries and invited guests assemble. As evening falls, they form a procession which follows the band up Main Street to St. Michael's Square where, from the deck of Danter's Waltzer's or Studt's Dodgems (now owned by Danters), the Town Crier proclaims the 'Cry of the Fair'.

Following the church blessing, the Fair is officially opened by the Mayor and the Town Crier declares: "This Fair holds three days, God Save the Queen."

The opening of Pembroke Fair in front of the Wesleyan Chapel – the pitch that would have been occupied by Haggar's Bioscope.

Then the music starts up and the excitement in the gathered crowd mounts in a sea of sound and coloured lights. It is not hard to imagine the impact of the Fair long ago, in an age before electric light, when the lives of the townsfolk would have been transformed with light and sound.

How great must have been the spectacle of Haggar's Bioscope with its beautifully painted show front lit up with hundreds of sparkling lights and high kicking show girls in their short dresses dancing to the music of the Marenghi organ: they must have been spellbound!

My brother, Roy used to tell us an amusing story he had heard about a well known local tailor, who went by the nickname of Scissors Thomas. The story goes that he had once taken one of the Haggar dancing girls to the Commons Park with the intention of having a kiss and a cuddle; he was most perturbed when he realised that he was proposing to cuddle a man!

This man was most probably Henry Haggar who, as a youngster, would on occasion bedeck himself in one of his sisters' dresses and dance on the front of the show with them. He admitted this in a talk to Merthyr Rotary Club in 1936.

"On leaving school I again went into the business – this time to dance with my three sisters in front of the organ. I can assure you that competition in those days was very keen, especially when we used to meet the Dooners and Crecrafts at the Fairs. We used to put our shows up next to each other, and a great competition always took place for the best costumes and films."

The restored 'Maid of Cefn Ydfa' as seen at the great Dorset Steam Fair.

WILLIAM Haggar first purchased an electric generator in 1900 but it was heavy and cumbersome. The show was to greatly benefit with the acquisition of a traction engine a few years later in 1904.

This was the Showman's Engine no.9386 made to order for William Haggar by Fowler of Leeds, registration number AX 2857. He named it 'The Maid of Cefn Ydfa'.

The driver from Fowler Engineering who delivered the engine all the way from Leeds, was dumbfounded when William paid in gold. Rather hot under the collar, the driver demanded a police escort to protect him on the return train journey home with his gold-lined cash tin.

Henry Haggar also recalled this in his talk:

"As time went on, we purchased our first traction engine, which was delivered to Brynmawr and frightened the family with its huge size.

The arrival of this however meant that we could take most of the show with us by road to the towns visited and, what was perhaps more important still, it meant that we were able to generate electricity for lighting and projection.

This in itself in those days was enough to make people come to see the show just to see how the magic lights worked. Still, even the traction engine had its drawbacks, as was proved on one occasion when it ran away on Treharris Hill (Merthyr) smashing the glass fronts of two shops next to the corner where now stands the chemist's shop."

'Cymru am Byth' powering the Royal Electric Bioscope.

The engine was William's pride and joy. The advent of the showman's engine meant that electricity could be produced by the 'on board' dynamo which ran the projector and all the sparkling coloured lights on the front of the show, which people came from miles around to admire. Horses and trains were no longer necessary to transport the show around; it could be towed behind 'The Maid' from town to town, and all for the price of a couple of bags of Welsh coal.

Steam also made possible the bigger rides and changed the face of fairground entertainment. Before, amusements were hand-turned roundabouts, swinging boats and strikers where you would hit the pin with a heavy hammer to hit the bell at the top and such like amusements. The first mechanical rides were the switchbacks, the carousels and the much-loved Noah's Ark driven by steam, the mechanics of which would send the wooden animals up and down.

The coming of the Fair to the town was eagerly looked forward to. I have been told that the young lads of the town would go out and meet the fair beyond Penny Bridge, where all the steam engines would stop so as to get up enough steam to climb that hill. Following the fair into town was a real treat and great was the excitement on seeing those beautiful, highly polished steam engines.

WILLIAM was to buy another two traction engines: 'Cymru am Byth', Fowler 11045, built in 1907 and 'King George V', Fowler 11815, built in 1910.

The showman's engine 'King George V' became known as Walter's engine: it pulled Walter's Bioscope all over Wales, which he toured with his wife Ada and family. When, during WWI, traction engines were requisitioned by the War Office in 1915, it brought the days of the travelling show to an end. These two engines were taken to the Front to tow the big guns and never returned.

This was not, however, the fate of my great grandfather's first engine 'The Maid of Cefn Ydfa'. I love Steam Fairs and visit both the Welland and the Great Dorset Steam Fair every year. Imagine my delight in seeing 'The Maid', which has now been painstakingly restored by Gerald Williams and Sons of Ledbury on Wye. I can claim to be the first Haggar to have stood on its footplate for over 100 years!

Gerald told me that he took a chance in bidding for some boxes, purported to contain a steam engine, at an auction. He did not even know if the engine was intact. After he and his boys had done a rough assembly job they realised that all the bits were there and began restoration in earnest. They have done a wonderful job and 'The Maid' now stands proud in the line-up at the steam fairs.

On my first visit to the Great Dorset Steam Fair in 2013, I was absolutely stunned when, all of a sudden, I was standing in front of a Bioscope almost exactly resembling the pictures I had seen of my great grandfather's shows. I did not think I would ever see such a thing on a showground: it was as if the past had come to life!

Walter Haggar's engine 'King George V'.

Along the front of the show was the history of William Haggar displayed on interpretation boards and, whilst looking at these in a state of euphoria, a gentleman, Richard Dean, appeared. I introduced myself and he was as amazed to see me, a member of the Haggar family, as I had been to see his bioscope.

Richard showed me around the Bioscope and told me he had long had a fascination with William Haggar. His son Tom demonstrated the workings of the fairground organ and showed me the concertina folded music books. These were fed into the organ to operate the pipes to produce the music.

Richard told me that everything in his show was authentic; he used an old cinematograph projector and only ever showed original silent movies. Just as in Haggar's day, the show began with Richard playing Master of Ceremonies, sporting top hat and tails.

Restoring the legend... Dean's Bioscope at Dorset Steam Fair.

Then the bevy of beauties, the paraders or dancing girls, took to the stage exactly as they did all of those years ago dancing to the music of the fairground organ, recreating something of the magic of Haggar's Bioscope in the early 1900s.

The ornate show front and organ of Dean's Bioscope are the work of Richard's family business, a professional organ building company based in Bristol.

Richard only ever builds his bioscope up at the Great Dorset Steam Fair and it was such a thrill to experience a spectacle that, previously, I was only able to imagine.

Chapter 7
Will Haggar Jnr Opens the Pembroke Cinema

HAVING been a main attraction at Pembroke Fair for many years, the Haggars were no strangers to Pembroke. They also shot many films locally; as Walter tells us in his memoirs they would often travel to Pembrokeshire in the summer months when the weather was fine.

Although their days of fairgrounds and film making had passed, a new chapter in the Haggars' association with Pembroke was to come in the early 1930s when my great uncle William Haggar Jnr. (who I shall refer to as Will) and his wife Jenny Lindon opened Haggars Cinema in Pembroke Main Street.

Will had always been an actor. Right from a boy, he was with the original Haggar's travelling theatre and later, with his wife Jenny Lindon, played the halls throughout the country. When his father went into the cinema business, Will took over the travelling theatre which was also to provide the actors for his father's groundbreaking, fictional films the first of which was *The Maid of Cefn Ydfa* in 1902.

Prior to World War One, William Haggar's film making came to an end with the disbanding of Will's theatrical company, which had provided all the assets for the production of his films. With great reluctance Will had entered the cinema business at last, substituting films instead of plays in his Castle Theatre in Pontlottyn which burnt down in January 1914.

Their new Castle Theatre Picture House moved to the former skating rink in Pontardulais but when history repeated itself and this also burnt down in 1923, Will returned to acting, touring the Halls.

This was not to prove successful – he was a Victorian actor and somewhat time-honoured; he finally gave up the acting profession to return to the cinema business.

Possibly because of happy associations with Pembroke, Will and Jenny decided to set up their cinema in the old Assembly Rooms in Main Street, which they leased from a Mr Rees Phillips and where a cinema had run intermittently since 1920.

The first cinema in Pembroke was actually situated on the North Quay in Ford's Yard opposite the castle.

It was not a permanent structure but a grounded Bioscope belonging to Gideon Roberts and his wife Sarah (nee Ford), whose daughter Ada had married Will's brother, Walter. They stayed there during 1914 and 1915, providing their own electricity with their portable steam traction engine.

THE ASSEMBLY Rooms in Main Street had been purchased by Rees Phillips from the Pembroke Assembly Rooms Company Ltd. which built it in 1866. It was opened on the 21st March 1867.

The Assembly Rooms had been built as a centre for the social activities of the town and, during its life-time, had served a variety of purposes including a drill-hall and shooting range for the 4th Battalion Welsh Regiment (volunteers) and the headquarters of the British Legion.

On the first floor there was a ballroom and on the floor above, a Masonic temple. The ballroom was an elegant structure, modelled on the Pump Rooms in Bath, with much moulded plaster-work, gold leaf, tall elegant pilasters crowned by coats of arms and vast ornate gold framed mirrors.

Pembroke Main Street showing the gable-fronted Assembly Rooms a few doors up the street from the clock tower.

Kelly's Directory describes it thus:

The Assembly Rooms, built by a company in 1866, consist of a large hall capable of holding 400 persons, lobbies, and a hall and tea room over the hall, so arranged that when occasion requires they can be thrown into one; the hall is let for public meetings and entertainments.

I have not been able to ascertain the exact date when the Assembly Rooms were purchased by Rees Phillips (possibly during or immediately after WWI) and it would seem that, in around 1920, he installed a ciné-projector in the ground floor hall which he proceeded to advertise as Pembroke Cinema.

He placed advertisements in Ward-Davies' *Free Press and Economic Advertiser* which would comment on the films being shown eg.

There is a good film showing at the Assembly Rooms this evening in which Henry Edwards and Chrissie White, those popular English film artistes, are featured. The production, entitled 'Alwyn', has a beautiful Welsh setting, and is a story that grips throughout.

Performances are nightly at 7.30 and on Saturdays three performances at 3, 6.30 and 8.30. (July 8th 1921)

Rees Phillips, however, was running a successful cabinet making business at 40 Main Street and he subsequently leased out the hall.

Later in the same year we see, from advertisements in that same periodical, that the cinema was under the management of Wil L Cotton who is described as 'Lessee and Manager'.

His shows comprised a mixture of live entertainment and films; for example an advert in the October 14th 1921 edition announced a special attraction:

Tom Owen, the original Welsh comedian presents 'Rare-Bits', the finest Concert Party travelling. In addition the following pictures will be shown: 5th episode of 'Diamond Mystery' Pathé's Gazette, Bray's Famous Pictorial etc.

Book your seats at the Cinema daily – 2s, 1s 3d, 9d (including tax). Children's matinee on Saturday at 2 o'clock.

BUT this was not to last: in *Kelly's Directory* of 1923 we see John Usher as proprietor and not long afterwards the cinema ceased to be.

We learn from the Pembroke Town Guide of 1926 that the Assembly Rooms were still the venue for concerts, public meetings, theatrical performances and dances but, if you wanted to see a movie, you had to go to the Grand Cinema in Pembroke Dock *a well-appointed picture house which exhibits up-to-date talking films. Buses leave for Pembroke after each performance.*

However, the cinema revived in 1927. *The West Wales Guardian's* edition of December 23rd 1927 reported

***Cinema, Pembroke.** – The proprietors of the Cinema, Pembroke, are reaping a good reward in their enterprise in re-opening this place of entertainment, for good audiences have been the rule for the last week or two, and the splendid programmes and tuneful orchestra are much appreciated.*

For the remainder of the week, the chief picture will be 'Shadows of Paris' featuring Charles Ray, and on Monday for three days, 'Flames' will be the star attraction.

In this picture the forest fire in natural colours is an outstanding feature. Those patrons who have not visited the Cinema this week will be interested to know that the new chairs have been installed.

IT WAS at this time of change in the cinema, which saw talking pictures and the beginnings of colour films, that Will Haggar leased the cinema from its proprietor Rees Phillips and named it Haggars.

It was to be the beginning of a family business that lasted 50 years through three generations. Many of the features from the 'old show' were retained and installed in the Pembroke Cinema. Two of the carved figures, known as 'The Teak Ladies', which had stood on either side of the fairground organ of the old bioscope frontage, were displayed in floodlit alcoves on either side of the cinema screen resplendent in their gold-leaf decor.

Other features retained were the pay box, the operating box, the spool box and the re-winding machine. There was an entrance on either side of the seating area, as was a feature of the old bioscope, and the heavy drape curtains across entrance passageways and emergency exits were drawn at the beginning of the show.

Will and Jenny had spent the best years of their lives on the stage and were beloved by audiences throughout Wales. Will Haggar Jnr. was a fine man and an impressive actor in the Victorian tradition, possessing a resonant voice and always dressing flamboyantly in his red lined cape and homburg, carrying a silver headed cane and sporting a button hole in his lapel.

WHEN the Haggars took over the cinema in the town, the programme would have been a mixture of live entertainment and films. Although the 'talkies' were by then making their mark, silent movies were still being screened; apparently it was not unknown for the couple to stand behind the screen and provide the dialogue.

Although 1927 had seen the release of *The Jazz Singer*, the first feature length 'talking film', the silent films did not go silently; several years passed before their eventual demise.

When Will and Jenny first came to Pembroke they found lodgings for a short period with Mrs Elsdon at Trewent House, almost opposite the cinema. A local resident, Mrs Dilys Hanmer, lived nearby as a child at no. 18 Main Street (now the present Williams' restaurant). She can remember the Haggars well, as Will would often wave to her from the window opposite and she recalls Jenny putting a flower in his lapel every evening before he went over to the Show.

They later purchased a house at 8 Merchants Park, where I remember going to see my Aunt Jenny and her daughter Josephine, who was also an actress.

On the right is Haggars Cinema in Main Street, 1935.

Will and Jenny had six other children: Jennie, Gladys, Phyllis, Dorothy, Billy and Patrick. The Pembroke Cinema was, as always, run as a family concern, all children helping to run the show. I have spoken to several local people who can remember, with some amusement, Patrick going around Pembroke swathed in bandages to advertise the film *The Invisible Man*.

William Haggar Jnr. and his family contributed a great deal to the cultural life of Pembroke and gave unstinting support to the amateur dramatic and operatic groups in the area. In 1935 they organised the Pembroke Silver Jubilee Pageant.

Will died in 1935 at the age of 64 and was buried in St. Daniel's Cemetery, Pembroke with his son, Patrick who died tragically in the same year at the age of 22. Jenny was buried with them after her death in 1954.

William's obituary

THE late Mr Haggar was a native of Yarmouth and was in his 64th year. It was in the South Wales district that he worked and lived and became known and respected.

During his lengthy visits to the various towns he made many friends and it speaks much for his popularity and integrity that he could be sure of a welcome, hearty and sincere, in any place where he had once set his foot,

Acknowledged as an ideal leading man, he had played most of the great parts – Shakespearean and others. With his fit-up

Will Haggar Junior and Jenny Lindon in Pembroke.

theatre he travelled most of the fair grounds, as well as appearing in the leading theatres.

The coming of the cinema, of which the deceased's father was a pioneer, was a severe blow to the family. The consequence was that, like others of showland, Mr Haggar relinquished the stage and entered into the management of Pembroke Cinema.

British Film Institute

Chapter 8
Walter Haggar

AFTER Will's death, the cinema was run for a short time by his widow Jenny and then by his brother Walter Haggar, my grandfather.

Walter was no stranger to Pembrokeshire, where Haggars was a popular fairground attraction as well as a favoured location for film making. He also operated Haggar's Electric Coliseum in Puss Hall Fields at the top of Frederick Street, Neyland from 1915-1919 when his traction engine 'King George V' was requisitioned by the War Department leaving him marooned on site.

The Haggar's Electric Coliseum, brightly lit with Hagger (instead of Haggar) displayed in large letters across the wooden canopy, was to remain active on this site until 1920 when a permanent show was erected. Walter describes this in his memoirs:

"My own travelling cinema came to rest at Neyland, Pembrokeshire, in the fall of the year 1915. We put in a wooden floor, built a wooden roof and gave the customers better seating. We installed central heating, sold the organ and put in a gas engine to generate electricity as my traction engine had gone off to help defend the country. We were firmly established as a local cinema and there I stayed during the whole of the First World War, opening the show every night under very trying conditions, such as shortage of labour and the non-arrival of film.

I was finally left with one boy to assist me and we managed to carry on until March 20th 1920 when my cinema was sold to Jimmy Harding, a local resident and fish buyer of Milford Haven Fish Market.

I then moved to Aberdare and joined my brother Henry in partnership. We took over the permanent cinema which father had built to replace his travelling cinema."

When his father died, Walter inherited the Kosy Kinema in Aberdare but he sold it in 1927. He moved his family to 38, King George Avenue, Bournemouth and took over the old cinema in Fordingbridge, which he later demolished and rebuilt.

He came to Pembroke in 1937 to take over the management of Haggar's Cinema when his widowed sister-in-law Jenny decided she could no longer cope with running it alone, leaving his Fordingbridge cinema in the care of his son, my father Leonard Haggar.

My grandmother Ada Haggar (nee Roberts) was also born into show business and her father Gideon Roberts, as previously stated, had run a 'grounded Bioscope' at Ford's Yard on the North Quay in Pembroke 1914-15.

My grandpa Walter and Ada were married in Aberdare in 1906. She was one of 13 children all brought up on the showground. Two of Ada's sisters, Frances and Lily, married Dorset-based showmen Edgar and Bill Symonds. Their marriages related the Haggar family to many fairground families such as the Shufflebottoms, the Booths and the Locks.

When Walter came to Pembroke, he and my grandmother were living apart for Grandpa, a rascal with a roving eye, had set his sights upon another lady whom we knew as Miss Bailey. However, he and Ada had brought up five children together (Grace, Madge, Leonard, Roy and Mary) and were still friends. When I was a young girl, we often visited her at her home in Bournemouth.

Walter cocks a snook in a scene from 'The Life of Charles Peace', filmed in Pembroke Dock.

I remember my grandpa Walter as always smiling, sticking his tongue out at us, pulling funny faces 'gurning' at us or 'cocking a snook' at someone or other: he was always clowning around and I don't ever remember him being serious. I can still see him wearing a check shirt, a red and white neckerchief, baggy corduroy trousers with braces, plimsolls with no laces and sometimes an old straw hat: he obviously had a business suit but I wasn't around to see that!

When we were little, he used to take us down the garden of our house in Pembroke, sit us all in a circle and tell us funny stories, some of them a little bit on the naughty side. He was a dear soul and we all loved him very much.

Mum and Dad were trying to bring us up to mind our 'Ps and Qs' and to behave correctly in public. 'Don't talk with your mouth full' etc; but Grandpa, or 'Pa' as he was known by our elders, was determined to make us laugh with our mouths full and, at the end of every meal, he would demonstrate how to lick your plate in a most ostentatious way – more than our backsides were worth to try that one!

On one occasion, when he was challenged about this, his reply was: "But you've never been starving, have you?"

I used to love watching him entertain us with his Irish dancing but my favourite was when he used to play the spoons; he was very good at doing that!

Although Grandpa was a comedian both on and off stage, he was in fact a very clever man and right from the beginning of William Haggar's experiments with film and film-making, he was always at his father's side, always ready to grasp new ideas as well as being an accomplished actor and musician.

Walter Haggar in his acting days.

Grandpa Walter acted in many of his father's films. In 1905, aged 22, he starred in *The Life and Death of Charles Peace*, a film about a notorious Victorian murderer. It still survives and is in fact the oldest extant British story film.

Almost all of the parts were played by members of the family and it was filmed in Pembroke Dock, mostly in Hawkestone Road, Birdcage Walk and the Railway Station. For the making of this film the Station Master and his staff allowed him to use the train and the station, and also played a part in helping the police to catch the wily Charlie.

A lady loaned her house for the burgling scene and local townsfolk played the crowd scenes. In the film you see Charlie trying to escape from a moving train; a dummy was used for this scene but when it came to the 'hanging' it was the real thing! The actual 'drop' was for real and Walter was nearly choked to death – it was a very narrow escape!

Walter and his partner were later to move to a bungalow in Manorbier. Walter had been deemed unfit to run the cinema after having let an entertainment tax inspector into the show half way through the performance for one shilling and without a ticket – he was prosecuted for not paying entertainment tax, of eight and a half pence on a one and nine penny ticket!

This resulted in my father and mother, Len and Pam Haggar, having to leave their home in Fordingbridge to take over the running of the Pembroke cinema.

My brother Roy was the only child then and was aged six. He used to tell us that he was given the job of buying the entertainment tax stamps at the Post Office and sticking them on the tickets. How he hated the taste of the glue!

Roy was close to his grandpa and often stayed with him at his Manorbier home. I remember him telling me about one of those occasions. Walter loved his flowers and had grown some prize daffodils in his garden but, unbeknown to his grandpa, Roy picked the heads off these precious flowers. Roy was so upset when he realised the seriousness of what he had done that Miss Bailey had to 'make it all right' by sewing the flower heads back on the stems!

Grandpa (left) lived in Manorbier until the mid 1940s. He then returned to Alderholt in Hampshire where he lived for the rest of his life and spent many happy years running the Haggars Cinema in Fordingbridge.

On his retirement he handed the cinema over to his son Roy Norman Haggar, a Spitfire pilot during the War years.

Uncle Roy was also running the Haggars Cinema in Lyndhurst but came to Pembrokeshire in the early 1960s where, for a short time, he ran the Manorbier Camp cinema.

Chapter 9
Leonard Haggar

WHEN my father Leonard, or Len as he was always known, moved to Pembroke in 1939 with his wife Pam and son Roy, they made their home in Main Street at 64 Orielton Terrace. As the providers of entertainment in the town, Mum and Dad soon became popular members of the community.

Shortly after taking over management of Haggars, Len began negotiations to purchase the cinema premises, which had previously been leased, and then proceeded to renovate the building to create a modern cinema.

The exterior of the building was spruced up, redesigned and repainted. The small side entrance door and over-door canopy were replaced by a wide, recessed front entrance with a canopy which extended across the pavement along the whole width of the frontage. It was fitted with many coloured lights and the name 'Haggars', in big white letters, appeared right across it.

Later, as the traffic in the Main Street increased and vehicles got taller and larger, the canopy, which hung over the pavement, had to be reduced in depth to prevent vehicles hitting it. The shortened canopy was enhanced with hanging baskets so as not to lose any of its impact. Len was always very proud of his baskets and their maintenance was high on his list of priorities.

Besides replacing the seating, a new screen was installed along with new curtains which had an automatic opening and closing device. The ceiling was repainted and concealed lighting installed.

The operating box was re-vamped and two new Kalee projectors were put in place. Films were made up of so many reels in those days that one projector was not sufficient to keep the show rolling.

In many cinemas with only the one projector, the audience was faced with a blank screen whilst reels were changed. At Haggars, someone had to watch the 'cue' spots on the film at the end of each reel in order to switch over at the right moment to ensure projection continuum.

Len Haggar's taking over management of Haggars, Pembroke coincided with the outbreak of WWII in 1939.

*Grandma Ada with young Len
and sisters Madge and Grace.*

There could not have been a better time to do so. Pembroke Dock saw a great influx of troops, the Dockyard was vibrant with activity and this influx of servicemen into the area assured full houses at Haggars.

Providing entertainment to raise morale excused my father from joining the armed forces, although he did serve by becoming a part -time fireman – which was to prove a perilous occupation – and a member of the Royal Observer Corps.

Although Pembroke emerged unscathed after WWII, its proximity to Pembroke Dock, an important garrison and dockyard town, meant bombing was not far away. I wasn't around when war started and my only memories are of dad in his uniform, the siren, the gas mask and the cellar where we used to shelter in the time of air raids.

My brother Roy, though, was a young boy and his memories of these times were vivid; memories which have fortunately been captured in a recorded interview by Linda Asman, of the Pembroke and Monkton Local History Society. One particularly bad raid that Roy recalled was the bombing of the oil tanks at Llanreath, Pembroke Dock on August 19th, 1940.

"Everyone in Pembroke remembers the day the tanks were bombed. I was down the park with my mother and my brother John was in the pram. I saw this aircraft coming in and then a bomb coming out of it – then this great eruption of flames and smoke.

My mother was very upset and hurried us home, immediately taking us into the cellar as we had a bomb shelter in there. My father came running in, grabbed his uniform and that was the last we saw of him for about four days as he was off with the AFS (Auxiliary Fire Service) to tackle the burning tanks which, as you know, burned for three weeks – and spotted all the apples and my mother's washing."

Haggars in the 1940s with new entrance.

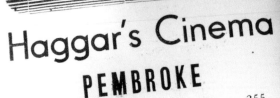

Haggar's Cinema
PEMBROKE

'Phone: 255.

RECENTLY MODERNISED AT GREAT
EXPENSE, AND IS FITTED WITH

R.G.A. SOUND SYSTEM

PERSONAL MANAGEMENT INDICATES
PERSONAL ATTENTION TO ALL PATRONS.

ALWAYS A GOOD SHOW AT HAGGAR'S

Lessee and Manager: L. W. HAGGAR.

HAGGARS CINEMA PEMBROKE

MONDAY, August 7th—
At 5.30 and 7.30.   One Show Tuesday and Wednesday at 7.15

MERLE OBERON AND GARY COOPER IN

THE COWBOY AND THE LADY

AND FULL SUPPORTING PROGRAMME

THURSDAY, August 10th—
Two Big Films in One Programme—By Special Request

SCARFACE AND HELL'S ANGELS

Thursday and Friday at 7.15.   Saturday at 2.30, 5.30 and 8.30

THE NEW ENTRANCE WILL BE OPEN TO THE PUBLIC at 5.15 on Monday

Adverts for Haggars Cinema. The one on the right is from 1939 and notes the unveiling of the new entrance.

In his book *Inferno 1940* Vernon Scott recalled that fateful day:

Regular fireman Eddie Jones received the message at 3.30pm and didn't waste a second. He raced out of the office and yelled to the knots of waiting firemen: "It's the tanks! We're on our way. Let's go, let's go."

Among his crew was Pembroke cinema proprietor Len Haggar. As the fire engine nosed impatiently out onto the Main Street watched by a large and anxious crowd, he spotted a man gesticulating wildly. It was the cinema's head projectionist, Harold Smith.

"He was dancing about like a madman," Haggar would remember afterwards. "He kept shouting that if he didn't have the bloody keys to the bloody cinema, there wouldn't be any pictures that night. I tossed him the keys from the moving fire engine. He caught them, grinned and gave the thumbs up sign. It was just as well he remembered the keys because I wouldn't enter my cinema again for another three weeks."

David Neville in his book *Bright Sparks* printed my father's recollection of *seeing a line of fireman turning like chickens on a spit. It was so hot they could not stand still for more than a few seconds.*

Roy's interview continued:

"The nights following the tanks' raid, they bombed Pembroke Dock heavily. I was in Pembroke so I was comparatively safe, although I didn't know it. The sounds were terrifying. We had a Morrison shelter – I think it was a Morrison Shelter – in the cellar and my father tunnelled a hole through the rock into the next house so that if we got trapped we could get through.

I slept in this hole and we used to store apples down there, wrapping them in paper and putting them on top of the Morrison shelter and so, for years after, if ever I heard the siren I smelt apples and cement dust."

Len in his AFS uniform with wife Pam, Roy and baby John.

There were humorous moments too:

"My father was on duty at the top of St. Daniel's Hill and old man Campbell was at the bottom of the hill. Several car loads went through and my father noticed they were a bit alien in shape. Eventually an army major turned up on his way to Castlemartin: 'Who let that bloody old fool loose, you'd better go down, he's going to kill somebody!'

And they went down and found that old man Campbell was getting people out of the cars and making them line up with their hands in the air. (Roy chuckled) Terrifying with his rifle!!

He didn't run the garage in my day; Ronnie Campbell ran it when I was a youngster and he had the old fashioned petrol pump with the glass on the top and cars used to stop there to get their petrol.

He ran two American cars (which were Chryslers, like gangster cars) and these were used to tow the pumps for the Auxiliary Fire Service, which was based in the Town Hall in Pembroke; Pembroke branch, that was. The AFS became the National Fire Service and it was the AFS which went into action at the time of the tanks, and before that with the raids on Pembroke Dock.

Into the area came service men and women from all over Britain and the Empire - Czechs, Poles, Dutch and then the Yanks.

Auxiliary Fire Service in training. Len Haggar is on the right.

The first time I saw Americans, they marched into Pembroke Main Street where I was standing with Colonel Beddoe who used to run the ironmongers opposite the cinema – he was an elderly gentleman who always wore a brown suit, a bowler hat and had grey moustaches.

These Americans came down the street, shuffling almost. Now we were used to British soldiers looking very smart but the Americans weren't as fussed and Colonel Beddoe (who'd been a CO in the old defensible regiment, the Welch Regiment) watched them pass.

'Huh!' he said. 'Soldiers!!' He snorted, turned around and marched back into his shop."

"WE, my mother with a pram and children, used to go out for a walk on Sunday afternoons up the Lower Lamphey road and on one occasion I remember Americans marching towards us.

The siren went and, to our astonishment, they all dived into the ditch – so my mother stopped and said: 'Why are you lying in the ditch?'

The Americans replied 'We're in the action zone ma'am.' They must have felt very foolish I think.

I must have been seven or eight when the Americans came; mind we loved the Americans. They were immense men, huge men and they brought chewing gum and fags, if you were so inclined, and they had an entertainments centre, what they called a USO, in St. Mary's Church Hall.

The kids used to congregate outside – 'any gum chum?' they'd say trying to get sweets. I had been told I wasn't to do it and I was out there one evening with my friends when my father came along, grabbed me by the scruff of the neck and I was marched off home and told off.

Anyway, I was out walking with my father through Pembroke not long after and there were two American officers, extremely smart in their uniforms, dark jackets and light coloured trousers. We were walking past when one of them offered me a bar of Cadbury's mint cream chocolate.

He'd taken one square off and I can see it now, the green cream dripping out of it, and he offered it to me. My father was ahead of me and I said 'no thanks'. He said 'go on, kid, you take it'.

I again refused and he said 'OK kid' and I went on.

My father said 'What did the American want?' and I proudly said 'He offered me a bar of chocolate'.

He said 'Did you take it?' 'No,' I said.

'Silly fool,' he replied.

I remember one very unpleasant incident. There were black Americans in Lamphey and they'd come into town and the white Americans chased them out. I can still see those black Americans screaming at them, running as fast as they could up the street as the whites chased them.

The other thing I remember is that they used to hire horses from Georgie Jenkins. I remember seeing Americans riding up Main Street and one particular one, fat, his legs sticking out and a cigar in his mouth.

They certainly created quite a stir when they came – they used to give us a Christmas party at St Mary's, a tremendous Christmas party with luxuries we hadn't seen since before the War."

American soldiers at the Pembroke War Memorial with Pembroke Mayor George Jenkins.

Chapter 10
The Wartime Cinema

TO QUOTE Roy Haggar: "Entertaining the troops meant busy times for Haggars during those wartime years: the cinema was a godsend to those men, a place of some warmth, comfort and entertainment in a bleak, bleak world.

The Sunderland crews of course were the elite. They would book the whole back row of lovers' seats, the two and nine pennies, and their favourite film was Disney's *'Goofy Learns to Fly'*."

Len used to keep a ledger of cinema income and expenditure and listed the films showing in the cinema that week. Throughout the war years, he made side annotations about the immediate happenings on the local and national fronts which make interesting reading.

Unfortunately I have only seen the ledger kept for the years 1940-41. It opened on March 31st 1940 and was marked 'Strictly Private' with the stern instruction 'This book is not to be shown to anyone connected with film returns, film renters or income tax authorities'.

Here are some examples of the entries.

Week ending June 1st 1940
Films showing: *Eternally Yours*, *Five Came Back*.
Note: British Expeditionary Force evacuated from Dunkirk with the loss of 30,000 men but 375,000 saved.

Week ending June 22nd 1940
Films showing: *Boy Slaves* (RKO Radio Pictures), *Oklahoma Kid* (Warner).
Note: France surrenders to Germany and Italy. I registered on Saturday. British Expeditionary Force comes home.

Week ending June 29th 1940
Films showing: *Alf's Button Afloat*, *Pygmalion*.
Note: Air raids on the county every night but no damage as yet. Second Marines gone away and Third Marines here. Am in the LDV [Local Defence Volunteers, later to become the Home Guard].

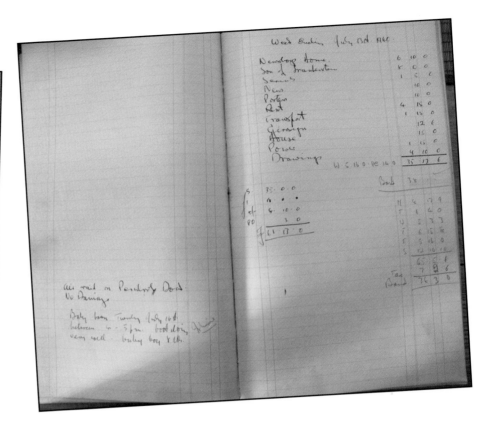

Above: Returns for week ending July 13th, 1940 noting the birth of a son, John.

Left: Len records the bombing of the oil tanks.

Week ending July 13th 1940

Films showing: *Newsboys Home*, *Son of Frankenstein*.

Note: Air raids on Pembroke Dock. No damage. Baby born Tuesday, July 16th between 4 and 5 pm. Both doing very well. Baby boy (Johnnie).

Week ending July 20th 1940

Films showing: *The Storm, Three Smart Girls Grow Up*.

Note: Some bombs dropped near me. Medical at Llanelli (Grade III).

Week ending July 27th 1940

Films showing: *Pacific Liner, Frankenstein and Dracula*.

Note: Bad air raid Monday, July 22nd from 12 midnight 'til 2am. Bombs dropped on Pembroke Dock and Milford. We were frightened somewhat.

Week ending August 3rd 1940

Films showing: *Way Down South, Chump at Oxford*.

Note: More air raids.

Auxiliary Fire Service

Week ending August 24th 1940

Films showing: *His Lordship Goes to Press, Doctor Rhythm.*

Note: 600 firemen arrived from London, Bristol, Cardiff, Llanelli, Birmingham etc. etc.

On Monday of this week 3 Junkers 88 dive bombers hit the tanks at Llanreath, Pembroke Dock which caused a big fire which is still burning today (Sunday). I have been down there with the Auxiliary Fire Service. Raiders returned and bombed and gunned the men.

5 men killed during the fire so far. More bombs today and during the week – in all they have hit the tanks 3 times. 5 tanks left from 16.

London, Portsmouth, Ramsgate and Southampton raided.

The aftermath of the oil tanks bombing at Llanreath.

Week ending September 7th 1940

Films showing: *Crime School, Tropic Holiday.*

Note: London bombed Saturday night, 400 killed. 1,800 injured.

Week ending September 21st 1940

Films showing: *Good Girls go to Paris, Angels with Dirty Faces.*

Note: More air raids. Full time AFS (Auxiliary Fire Service).

Week ending October 19th 1940

Films showing: *Let Us Live, The Spy in Black.*

Note: More raids and attack on Balloon Barrage and bombs on Pembroke Dock.

Romania occupied by Nazi troops.

Week ending November 9th 1940

Films showing: *Theodore Goes Wild, Pennies from Heaven.*

Note: Extremely heavy raids 6 am Tuesday. 36 x 500 lb. bombs dropped onto the docks. Numerous casualties, much damage - much wind up. No more since.

Greeks cut off Italian Division in Pindos Mountains.

Week ending November 16th 1940

Films showing: *You and Me, Professor Beware*.

Note: Terrible raid on Coventry. Town and Cathedral completely wiped out. 1,000 casualties.

Week ending May 24th 1941

Films showing: *Mexican Spitfire, Anne of Windy Willows, Vigils of the Night, Honeymoon Merry Go Round*.

Note: Germans land troops and equipment by air on Crete. Fierce battle now over and HMS *Hood* sunk off Greenland. *Bismarck* sunk.

Bomb drifted at Milton – road closed to traffic and large sub sunk by enemy aircraft in harbour off Milford.

Week ending May 31st 1941

Films showing: *Road to Singapore, Bulldog Drummond's Bride*.

Note: Into action under enemy fire this Tuesday night. Sharp attack – about 15 fires, Tanks nearly struck twice with High Explosives. I was in Bowlings, no casualties among our crew but two of the others killed. I was coffin bearer at funeral.

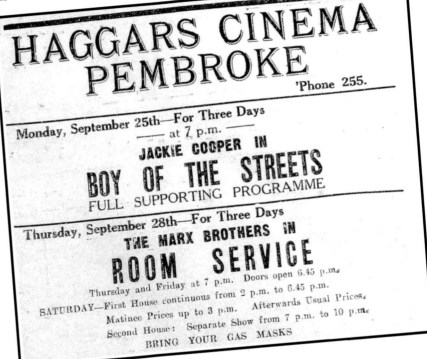

The show goes on – but 'Bring your gas masks'.
A wartime advert from the Western Telegraph.

Week ending August 9th 1941

Films showing: *The Sea Hawk* (Warner), *Shorts* (Warner), *The Roaring Twenties*, *Everybody's Happy*.

Note: All quiet.

Week ending September 20th 1941

Films showing: *Gangs of Chicago, Room for Two, Pastor Hall, John Smith Wakes Up* (British Lion).

Note: Was this week promoted to Section Leader NFS (National Fire Service) Pembroke.

Week ending December 6th 1941

Films showing: *Cross Country Romance, Saint's Vacation, Flight Angels, King of the Lumberjacks*.

Note: Big fire exercise this Sunday. About 500 men and 50 pumps at Llanion and Llanreath. Started at 5.30am and ended 10.30pm. Hard day.

Strictly private!

FORTUNATELY Len Haggar came through the war unscathed and, despite the bombings, the show went on and the cinema operated as normal.

However, operating the cinema would appear to have been a more hazardous occupation than fighting fires, as Roy was later to write:

"One night I will never forget, the film was 'In Which we Serve', a wartime drama concerning Lord Mountbatten's ship HMS Kelly, starring Noel Coward. In the film, the Kelly is torpedoed. I was in the cinema engrossed in the action: as the torpedo tore into the hull of the Kelly, the cinema screen went black and then red.

I knew immediately what had happened and ran around to the back of the cinema, where the operating box was a blazing inferno.

To my relief, my father staggered through the door, his hair singed and eyebrows gone but otherwise unharmed.

Our ancient, Simplex projector had run hot and the highly inflammable nitro film had exploded.

The irony was that my father, an auxiliary fireman, had come through the Blitz and the oil tanks fire without a scratch."

Chapter 11
The Post War Years

My Family

I WAS born in 1942, the third of six children. Roy, the eldest, was born in Bournemouth whilst John, myself, Tony and Susan came into the world when the family were living at 64, Main Street. Dinah, the youngest, was born after we moved to Little Barnard House at 122 Main Street. We needed a bigger house!

When we moved there, the house was derelict – gas chandeliers, old ranges, even servants' bells. The gardens were all overgrown and there were the remnants of a steam mill, cow stalls and a pig sty but my father, being a very industrious man, set about transforming it into lawns and flower beds.

It was especially exciting as we had, at the bottom of the garden, Barnard's Tower. At school we were taught that a big battle was fought there during the 17th century Civil War and to prove it we used to find musket balls!

Mum and Dad with Roy (centre back) and John, Tony and Vicki.

We loved it there and I have happy memories of playing in our 'castle' and of boating on the Mill Pond.

One thing dad was very fond of was his motor car and I think we had a new make and model almost every year. I remember the old Armstrong Siddeley, the Rolls-Royce, the Vauxhall Cresta, the Morris 1000, the Rover 90 and many more, too numerous to mention.

We used to go out every Sunday in the car to the local beaches where we would all walk along the sand and run up and down the dunes.

Dad also took us for walks around the town and, through him, I got to know all of the businessmen and shopkeepers; Walter Simon, Mr Gwilliam (otherwise known as Billy 2 Sticks), George Wheeler, Mr Mendus, Owen Lowless, Sid Brown and Les Stevens

Vicki, Tony and the Rolls outside 64 Main Street.

to name but a few, and even the film travellers who came to the house to arrange the films that were to be shown at Haggars for the next several months.

Dad was a member of the Showman's Guild and the family had very close connections with showmen all over the country.

Dad loved Pembroke and took a leading part in the community. He was a Town Councillor, Grand Master of the Free Masons and a member of the Rotary club; during his term as President (1958-1959) he presented the club with an engraved silver neck chain which is still worn by successive presidents.

Although he was offered the position of Mayor of Pembroke, he had to decline due to the commitment to his business.

My mother was also very active in the community; she was in the Inner Wheel, the Friends of the Hospital and helped at many events and functions in the town.

For three generations the entertainment gene was strong in the family and my father – 'the old man' as he was fondly referred to by his sons – himself experienced life on the road as a young man and knew how to entertain an audience.

But it was my brother Roy who inherited that ability to act in our generation: with a voice like Richard Burton as well as good looks, he could well have made a career in acting.

As a young man, Roy worked in the cinema with Dad for a while and, although it was the family tradition for the eldest son to inherit the business, in Roy's case this did not happen.

Being born into a famous theatrical

Len Haggar as President of Rotary.

family had instilled in him the desire to become an actor, but Dad and Grandpa Walter persuaded him that there were far more rewarding ways of earning a living than treading the boards.

Roy heeded their advice and focused his talents on education, but it was not too long before his ability as an amateur actor was recognised. He took part in several productions with the Tenby Players and, whilst teaching, directed or co-directed two school plays every year.

There was one production that both Roy and my father took part in and I mention it here because it was such a massive production that it is still remembered: The Pageant of Pembroke.

This amazing event took place over three days in 1958 and was organised by the Pembrokeshire Local History Society to commemorate the 500th anniversary of the birth of Henry Tudor in Pembroke Castle in 1457.

Roy as Henry VII in The Pageant of Pembroke.

The Pageant was postponed a year to coincide with the Festival of Wales in 1958 and became one of its biggest attractions. Written by Roland Matthias, an author and poet who at that time was Headmaster of Bush Grammar School, it told the story of Pembroke from Norman times to the Battle of Bosworth when Henry VII defeated Richard III and was crowned King of England.

It was a county-wide production, the enormous cast numbering around 600 drawn from all over Pembrokeshire and from all walks of life. Scenes were interspersed with ballet choreographed by Miss Violet Ellis (my ballet teacher from Penvro House in the Main Street, where she ran her ballet school). Mary Mendus and Dorothy Woodhouse advised on the production; Mollie Thomas advised on costume design and great numbers were involved in their making – everyone joined in!

To quote a contemporary account in the 'Western Telegraph': *Solicitors took their place in market day crowd scenes; housewives became rose maidens; schoolteachers discarded their normal garb to don drab, loose-fitting peasant costume; and shipyard workers joined forces with ministers of religion to take up battle stations as knights in shining armour.*

It was Roy who took the starring part of Henry VII. He wore an heraldic tunic over chain mail, an armoured helmet and had to ride a horse for the first time.

This was a local white cart horse which, much to Roy's embarrassment, decided to water the Gatehouse flagstones every time he made an entrance.

Apart from that, the horse – which normally undertook council haulage duties pulling a stout wooden cart around the town under the care of the carter, Eric Coleman – was very well behaved and beautifully groomed.

My father was a Burgher, as were other members of the council including Desmond Lowless, Charles Green and Alec Colley. He wore a long dark blue velvet gown and a black velvet hat, a bit like a tri-corn, and had a heavy chain bedecked with medallions around his neck that he had made from horse brasses.

Len Haggar (right) as a Burgher in The Pageant of Pembroke.

The Pageant of Pembroke drew an audience of thousands. It was a mammoth event that went down in history; everyone enjoyed it and it did the town proud.

The Cinema

AS CHILDREN we were all brought up in the cinema, helping out and being part of it.

The family grew quickly and, once able to stand on our own two feet, we were not left to our own devices for long – we soon became part of the business!

We all had the experience of 'showing people to their seats' taking care to hold the torch so that the light was directed to the floor and not in people's faces whilst looking for empty seats – and especially not to shine it on the lovers' seats in the back row! Then we took turns standing on the orange box in the projection room making sure that the arc lamps kept burning.

The family and the locals often talk about the days of the old projectors when the large number of reels called for split-second accuracy in watching the 'cue spots' and slamming from one projector to the other at the end of a reel. I remember that, if anything went wrong and the screen went black, you could hear the stamping feet of the audience which meant 'come on Haggar, get it right!'

During the war years, when power-cuts were frequent, this stamping, booing and hissing was a regular occurrence and the enthusiasm with which it was carried out showed that everyone was enjoying themselves.

In the event of a loss of power Len would leave the operating box and make haste to the generating room below to swing the generator (which he always called Jenny) into action in order to provide essential power to continue running the show.

Len always came out with perspiration on his forehead making it very obvious that this task was very exacting and required an awful lot of effort. In the mid 1970s the old Kalee projectors were replaced with Xenon Lamps, which made the job in the operating box a lot easier. Five reels could be spliced and put onto one spool, thus showing the whole film.

Most of us children served as ice cream sellers. There was always an interval in the middle of the programme when one of us would appear with the ice cream tray around our neck; it was quite heavy and uncomfortable but full of all kinds of goodies.

My sister Dinah held the sales record: "One evening I was told to sell ice cream and the picture that night was a desert one, Lawrence Of Arabia or something like that. I didn't really know what to do so I just went up to people and said 'Do you want an ice cream?' Of course, on the screen there were miles of sand and nothing but blazing heat. I think we broke the record on ice cream sales that night!"

'Eldorado' ice cream was a firm favourite.

Sweets were sold at the ticket office but we didn't like them very much. I remember John, Tony and myself sneaking out of the side door of the cinema, holding each other's hands in a crocodile, then crossing the road to Mrs. Elsdon's sweet shop in Trewent House to spend our sweet money. Then we'd sneak back unseen to our seats to watch the film.

We used to love Mrs. Elsdon's sweet shop, not only for the sweets but also because of Mrs. Elsdon. She had quite a white face, jet black hair, bright red lipstick and pointed features; we thought she was magic. We used to call her the Wizard of Oz and sneaking out to buy her sweets was always a naughty venture but great fun. She was actually my brother Tony's Godmother.

One advantage of having a cinema owner as a father was that we could get all of our friends a free seat. My sister Dinah was the biggest culprit and used to bring in half the school with her I think. I don't know if Dad knew what we used to get up to but he probably had a pretty good idea.

I was a lot older than Susan and Dinah and used to take them to the show when they were quite young. Sue remembers when I took her to see *Snow White* and she got so frightened by the witch that she cried her eyes out.

Nothing would pacify her and, as the rest of the audience were getting somewhat perturbed, we had to make a hasty exit. That little treat went horribly wrong!

Interior of Haggars Cinema. The 'Teak Ladies' from the Bioscope can be seen in the alcoves either side of the screen.

The post-war years were prosperous ones for Haggars. In those days of going to the pictures, the evening's entertainment was planned to give everyone, young and old, a chance to see the full show in a continuous performance.

The first film to be shown was the 'small film', a short feature film such as a comedy or short mystery, then the News (no television to see it on then) followed by the Pearl and Dean adverts. Then the main feature film, after which there was a repeat showing of the short feature film and the evening culminated with everyone standing to attention for the National Anthem.

We used to run out quick before it began but, once the strains of 'God Save the King' started to play, dare you move!

The programme ran from about 5.45pm to 10pm Monday-Saturday with a matinee on Saturdays and on wet days during the school holidays. These would be advertised on bill-boards outside the cinema and also over a tannoy system.

My father loved touring around the local highways and byways in his battered old Land Rover or A30 van with Sam, the Springer Spaniel, who sat proudly beside him listening to the well versed 'Matinee at Haggars' spiel.

Haggars Cinema in the 1950s.

Before the advent of television in the 1950s, so popular was the cinema that customers often used to queue right down to the Town Clock three or four people deep, waiting patiently for the doors to open. A 'cinema full' sign had to be displayed when all of the seats were gone and there were cinema goers standing down both sides of the auditorium.

Among the most popular films were the 'Carry On' series. These began in the late 1950s and were still going strong in the 70s.

Roy's daughter Sarah recalled the time she was with her grandfather whilst he was preparing his list of future film bookings to pass on to the film traveller – a list which included some more of the 'Carry On' films. She complained:

"Why don't you book some decent films grandpa? We don't want those old 'Carry On' films, why not book *Tommy*? Go on Grandpa, book *Tommy*!"

He turned to her and said, "Don't you ever knock those 'Carry On' films, they have kept this family in shoes for many a year."

Sarah now thinks back on what her grandpa told her many years ago. "It is not what you want that matters; it is what your audience wants and never forget that."

My brother Tony has vivid memories of our days helping out at the cinema in the fifties and sixties and these are recounted in the following chapter.

Sam the dog in the old Land Rover.

The Staff

MANY people were employed in Haggars and Dad was always very appreciative of his staff and talked fondly of them.

When he first started in Pembroke he took on a young lad to help him with odd jobs. This lad was a teenager named Eric Tunster who helped in the operating box and re-wound the films in the spool room; he died at a very young age and my father was very upset.

During the War years we had an operator called Harold Smith who was with us for quite a long time and who steadfastly kept the show open during the blitz on Pembroke Dock when Dad was engaged with fire-fighting.

Another henchman of my fathers was Brian (Ginger) Thomas who was an electrician at Castlemartin Camp. Every evening, Brian would turn up at The Show (as Dad liked to call it) dressed in shirt and tie, grey flannels and navy blazer. My dad having taken him under his wing at a fairly young age, Brian helped with any task asked of him and really felt a sense of belonging.

Dad and his Zephyr Zodiac with Dinah and Sue outside Little Barnard House.

Brian was brought up by his aunt in Station Road and really looked upon us as family friends; Dad supported him in every possible way and often gave him the job of relief projectionist. In return, Brian would never let the family down.

In no way can we forget the indomitable Tommy Griffiths of Orchard Buildings: Tommy was faithful to the end. Tearing tickets and keeping everything in order were Tom's main tasks, all the while keeping a keen eye on any impending problems upstairs and down.

Tommy had a very placid nature and a gentle but persuasive tongue; whatever the problem he would usually be able to sort things out and win the day. He was known all over the town and was very popular at the cinema.

After Haggars was gone and Tommy retired, he could invariably be seen sitting on the outside windowsill of The Railway Inn talking to all of his passing friends, many of them being Haggars' former patrons.

There were many usherettes employed through the years; those I remember are Gladys James, Betty Dudman, Jose Davies, Anita Davey, Barbara McCarthy, Dilys Cole, Shirley

Tommy Griffiths.

Clarke, Nellie Jordan, Betty Blunsden, Marjorie Dooley, Marjorie Wheeler and Diana Williams. Gladys also spent a lot of time as a cashier in the Pay Box as did Jackie Haggar and Diana Williams.

Mrs Gwyther was the faithful cleaner and also took her turn running the tea bar for upstairs entertainment. In latter years the cleaning job was undertaken by Molly Hancock who worked for Haggars for many years.

When Mum and Dad went off on holiday, my uncle Roy (who saw active service in the war years as a Spitfire Pilot and ran Haggars at Lyndhurst with his wife Anita) would come down to manage the Pembroke cinema.

Being a Haggar, he was well used to the world of the cinema so Dad had no worries. Marjorie Dooley, who was still in school whilst working at Haggars, remembers Roy fondly and told me he was always her favourite boss. Marjorie married John Goodman, who also did some work at Haggars in the 1950s.

John had the arduous task of working up a ladder in the cinema auditorium, washing the nicotine off the walls. The number of buckets of water John had to fetch was incredible; not the most pleasant of tasks but John stuck with it and did a brilliant job.

Those were the days when smoking was perfectly acceptable in public places – the walls would become absolutely yellow! Just think what it must have done to the lungs!

Dad had a small team of maintenance men – Mike Kucyj from the Ukraine, Herbert Uka, a native of Poland, who had served with the British Army and Otto Muller, a former German paratrooper who had been captured by the allies and served as a prisoner of war.

After the War they all married local girls and settled in Pembroke. Herbert was to marry Shirley Clarke who also worked at Haggars.

This multi-tasking workforce not only repaired the ballroom roof which was, according to Dad, the highest roof in town, but also undertook gardening, painting and decorating, cleaning, general building and maintenance work.

These tasks were not only confined to the show: they often helped out at our home with its enormous garden. My mother had several nanny/ home-helps: Patti Harding, Nellie Jordan, Dorothy Davies, Nancy Meaney, Anna Koder and Joan Lewis to name a few. Several of these ladies often helped out with various duties at the show as well.

We all remember Anna with a special fondness. She lived in as a member of the family and made us huge loaves of plaited bread, a secret recipe from her homeland, Germany. Anna was later to marry a local boy, Alan Smith, and they were to have two children, Zita and Roy.

Grandma Ada with Uncle Roy who sometimes ran the cinema.

Chapter 12
Tony's Tales by Anthony Haggar

Cinema Tales

OUR 'SHOW', as we referred to it, consisted of a cinema, dance hall and restaurant. This provided most of the entertainment for the quiet, if not always sleepy, Welsh town.

To the casual observer, the opportunity for a youngster like me to help to manage and run a cinema at that time, from the fifties to the seventies, must have seemed so exciting. However it was not all that it seemed. Many an amusing and calamitous incident arose in our 'Entertainments Emporium'.

Our cinema was powered by a complex set of machines. Located at the back of the cinema, in what we called the operating box, were the main projector and generator; this produced the high powered electric current needed for our arc lights, which projected the films to our anxiously awaiting audiences.

Our constant challenge, partly due to my father's philosophy that all money should be spent on the 'Front of the House' for the comfort of our audiences, was how to keep the ageing equipment functioning to make possible the showing of films.

Many a time when the audience was enthralled by John Wayne in *The Commancheros* or mesmerised by the beauty of Ingrid Bergman in *Casablanca* we were struggling with our ancient machinery 'to keep the Show on the road'.

So let me share some of my memories and amusing anecdotes, not only of the adventures of nurturing our machinery to continue but also of the other challenging issues for a young man born into the 'Entertainment Business'.

Listen to the Usherette

ONE of my earliest memories of the cinema happened when I was in primary school.

I cannot recall my exact age, but my father had begun to take me there on Saturday mornings to help him with various tasks. In those early days horror films were often crude and implausible. However, one film was attracting significant attention: *The Thing from Another World* produced by Howard Hawks.

One day my father eagerly described how the terrifying monster was making local audiences quake and my curiosity was immediately aroused! Off I trotted to the cinema the next day for the early performance, and attempted to sneak in by the side door.

Suddenly I was yanked back by the collar and asked by Nellie, the usherette: "What do you think you're up to?"

Nellie was a corpulent and formidable lady, of not inconsiderable gravitas, and could make a grown man wither with a single glance. What chance did I have?

"I've come to see the film Nellie," I bleakly explained.

"Tony, you're not old enough to see this, it's an 'X' film," she said glowering at me.

Foolishly I stood my ground, "My father owns the cinema and I can go in."

"Oh is that so?" said Nellie with a twinkle in her eye, "Well that's all right then isn't it; in you go."

I sat through the film absolutely petrified as the indestructible monster on screen created mayhem and havoc, with bodies strewn everywhere. I desperately wanted to flee from the cinema, but was too ashamed to face Nellie.

Just before the end of the film I slipped out and there was Nellie getting ready to go home. "Would you like me to walk you home Tony?" she asked, noticing my pale, quaking demeanour.

Nellie's and my home were in the same direction, but required us to walk about half a mile along the dark, lonely Main Street of Pembroke, with its ominous nooks, crannies and alleyways.

"Please Nellie," I shuddered.

Tony and John Haggar with Brian 'Ginger' Thomas (left).

We finally reached my house during which time I had imagined unmentionable things leaping out of dark passages behind me, ready to accost me in the most abominable way.

"Here we are," said Nellie, "home."

"Thanks Nellie," I said meekly and, "I'm also so very sorry for being cheeky to you."

"In that case," said Nellie, "I won't tell your father."

That night in my isolated bedroom, which was in a lonely annex of the dark house which I shared with my brother (who for some reason was away), I sat up all night quaking with my imagination running riot. Next day entering school (East End Primary) I felt tired and exhausted from my sleepless night. Our kindly headmaster Mr. Jones, noticing my distressed look, asked.

"Tony do you feel all right, you look as though you've seen a monster?"

Little did he know!

The trials and tribulations of the equipment

I BEGAN my career operating the cinema projectors at the tender age of eleven or twelve, when I used to help my father and Herbert or Mike, the permanent operators, during the performances.

The 'boy in the box' (as one was called) job ranged from feeding the arc lights (which would go out if not attended to every two minutes) to rewinding film reels after we had switched projectors.

The operating box at Haggars with its Kalee projector.

Most films consisted of four to five reels and each had to be rewound ready for the next performance. Unfortunately, at that age, I was not tall enough to see through the viewing aperture in the wall to ensure the film was progressing satisfactorily, so I was supplied with a large concrete block to stand on!

Often in those days we would suffer cuts in the mains electricity system, so all cinemas had a backup generating system. Ours consisted of an antiquated ex-army diesel engine, which was extremely noisy and vibrated so violently that it had to be housed in a separate generator hut.

True to form, during the opening of a new and popular film, I was busy at the projector when the mains electricity failed. I rushed immediately to start-up the emergency generator, which needed to be turned vigorously with a starting handle until it was spinning quite fast, then the compression lever was thrown and, with a bit of luck, the engine would cough into life.

At this stage you dashed back to the operating box, re-struck the arc lights, and the show commenced.

Needless to say this took a good five to ten minutes, during which time the audience usually took it upon themselves to make their presence felt, vigorously stamping their feet and howling delightedly.

On this particular night I had just restarted the performance when I noticed, as I switched from one projector to another, that the arc lights were dimming badly. This meant that our museum piece was struggling and I immediately ran back to the engine house to see what was wrong.

I then observed that the engine was overheating and emitting ominous black smoke.

On inspection, the radiator was short of water. I grabbed a nearby bucket and poured its contents straight into the radiator. What I hadn't realised was that the bucket contained the cleaning fluid 'Daz' that had been left there by a cleaner. When the engine began to spew large waves of froth from the radiator, I had a foreboding that all was not well and the likelihood of it lasting out to the end of the film was remote.

Urgent action was immediately required, but what? Thinking rapidly, I realised that the only way to complete the performance was to finish the film before the engine died which would mean I had to shorten the film! I had three reels to go, so I took the not so very executive decision to show only half of each reel which severely compromised the film.

It was lucky I did this because, just when the final scene came to an end, the strongly protesting generator gurgled and died. On showing the customers out of the cinema, a few of them remarked that the film seemed to be in an awful hurry to end: I just smiled obliquely wondering if I would ever be found out! But we did have a very clean engine room!

The joys of matinees

EVERY Saturday morning we showed a matinee for the local children. The matinee consisted of serials such as *Flash Gordon*, amusing shorts like *The Three Stooges*, a cartoon and usually a cowboy film;

Haggars Cinema programme cover, September 1956

SEPTEMBER 1956
*
H A G G A R'S
CINEMA
BALLROOM - CAFE
PEMBROKE
*
Proprietor : L. W. HAGGAR
Telephone : PEMBROKE 255
*
Monday, Thursday and Friday Continuous from 5.45. Tuesday and Wednesday, One Show only at 7 p.m. Saturday Continuous from 4.45 p.m.

Half-price Tuesdays and Thursdays only. The management reserves the right to refuse admission

Attractions

Among the favourites were 'Hopalong Cassidy' starring William Boyd and George 'Gabby' Hayes, despite him riding his horse in a very strange way whilst passing the same tree every few minutes.

Occasionally we showed a children's film from the British Film Institute which, in my view, was often superior to many adult films. One of our problems was controlling the children; they would all get terribly excited and screech at the tops of their voices whilst stamping their feet.

In one particular matinee, one of the 'baddies' in the film was about to do his dastardly deed, when a highly animated child chucked an ice cream at the villain and it stuck on the screen! My father, who had just replaced the screen at great expense for the new cinemascope films, was outraged.

He immediately stopped the film, brought up the lights and stomped onto the stage. Then he thoroughly berated the children asking them if they realised the cost of cinema equipment; threatening dire consequences should their misbehaviour continue! Silence prevailed to the end of the film.

At the end of the performance my father was still very upset and said we needed to do something to get some control over the children's behaviour in the matinees.

"Which kid is the biggest nuisance and has a propensity to moderate violence?" he asked. I told him and the following week we stopped this young tearaway.

He then said: "If you keep control of the other kids in the matinee you can have a free supply of ice cream."

Haggars in its heyday.

Not surprisingly, order was restored.

Ironically we could never get the ice cream mark off the screen and, for ever after, whenever a film was panning across a clear sky you could always see this ice cream floating through the air desperately seeking its elusive target!

Education, Education.

OCCASIONALLY, when a literary classic was made into a film, the Education Authority would commission the film for afternoon showings to the local schools. This happened when we were showing *Moby-Dick* starring Gregory Peck as Captain Ahab.

The book had been chosen for that year's school exams and the teachers and pupils were very keen to see this long and complex story on the silver screen. Mostly the teachers looked forward to the Hollywood interpretation; no doubt the pupils saw it as an opportunity not to read the book!

The film contained a very long speech made by Captain Ahab, which is reputed to have great literary merit and around which many examination questions would be asked. In this speech, Ahab nails a silver dollar to the ship's mast and addresses the ship's crew at great length, promising the sailors that whoever espies the great white whale would be rewarded with this silver dollar.

Bearing in mind that this rather long film had been showing twice nightly for a fortnight and we were now also showing it in the afternoons to the schools, my father had deteriorated to a gibbering wreck and was repeating this diatribe in his sleep.

Being a practical man, he had reasoned that local audiences would appreciate a sharper film with less literary merit, so he deftly cut the whole speech out of the film, with an intention of putting it back in for the schools' showings. But he forgot to do so.

At the next schools' performance the teachers were eagerly on the edges of their seats, no doubt believing that this deep and powerful novel, eloquently orated by the great Gregory Peck, would gently open their young pupils' minds to the joys of literature. Conversely my father (after his recent matinee experience) believed it was more akin to trying to forcibly open a rusty safe with a matchstick!

No sooner had Peck begun his verbose masterpiece than it was unceremoniously ended.

After the completion of the cut and shortened film, when my father was saying adieu to the schools, he was approached by a headmaster who soundly berated him that the film did not seem to contain this fine speech. My father, shame-faced, suggested that the headmaster may have missed it or perhaps fallen asleep during it.

Noticing the headmaster's complexion turning rather purple, he quickly changed tack, suggesting that you cannot really trust Hollywood to portray history or literature accurately.

The headmaster (being my headmaster) retorted by telling my father that if he was in his school, like his son (me), he would have ended up in detention with a very warm behind.

My father's humiliation and degradation was now complete, but I am sure I heard him muttering 'bloody intellectuals' under his breath.

Romance and the Cinema

IN THE cinema we had double seats placed in the back row, which were the favourite haunt for courting couples. It was probable that most of the local romances began in the back of the cinema, especially in the cold winter months.

However, the more mischievous of our usherettes would often shine their torches back there to embarrass the naive young Lotharios to create a little local exposé and supply them with ammunition for their imaginative gossip.

In my teenage years I was not averse to taking my girlfriend to the cinema (hooray, for free!) for a little kiss and cuddle.

However, it had some very severe disadvantages. Whenever I took a girlfriend to the cinema the usherettes would let my father know and, no sooner had I hesitantly put my arm around my beloved, than a light would shine on me and the usherette would whisper: "Tony your father would like to see you in the operating box."

At which stage I had to leave my poor girlfriend sitting in the cinema between the other courting couples. When I got to the operating box my father would say: "Tony can you take over just for five minutes?"

The result would always be the same. He never came back and I ended up completing the show, after which I also received a dressing down from my disgruntled girlfriend.

We had other amusing, or not so amusing, courting incidents and one stands out vividly in my mind. I was busy helping the cashiers and usherette (Daphne) at the ticket kiosk when we were approached by a local gossip, whose mouth was a disproportionate size to her brain.

"Daphne," she said, "I think you should go and check the back row, my dear," with a malicious look on her face.

Curiously I followed the usherette into the cinema to find out what was going on. She cast her torch along the back row and suddenly let out a piercing screech. "Henry!" she bellowed.

The usherette was no shrinking violet but rather a large and voluptuous lady. They say that "Hell hath no fury like a woman scorned" and, looking at the usherette's furious countenance, I had no doubt that this was a veritable truth.

She started flailing with her heavy torch and trying her best to get through the back row, ice creams and crisps flying everywhere.

Suddenly a rather green and panicky Henry, poor miserable creature, leapt out of his seat and, like a bat out of hell, streaked in the opposite direction as fast as his slippery feet would carry him. There were hoots of laughter from members of the audience and calls of "You're in trouble now Henry!"

It transpired that Daphne the usherette had exchanged shifts with her colleague and dear Henry did not realise his girlfriend would be on duty that night.

Needless to say, I never saw Henry in the back seats again!

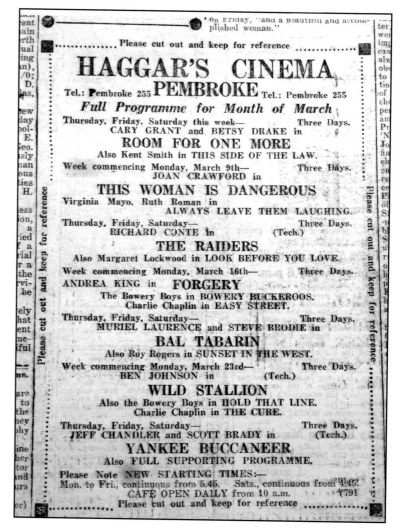

Who's providing the entertainment?

YOU will have gathered by now that our cinema was rather eccentric and unique, consequently showing films could at times be rather challenging.

At the opening performance of *The Robe* (the film of the year) starring Richard Burton, Jean Simmons, Victor Mature and Michael Rennie, my father emphasised that I needed to display my best artistic operating skills to enable the audience to fully appreciate the finer points of our art.

The cinema was full; we had a packed house. This was one of the first films to be shown in cinemascope and we had spent a small fortune on the new scope lenses. To show a film to its best advantage, a good operator will initially dim the cinema lights, start up the film with curtains closed, then slowly open them to create an impression of a wonderful event about to unfold.

Following these procedures and with the film already running, the curtains drew gingerly back but stuck half way! My heart sank, as this required me to rush through the cinema, run behind the screen and manually wind the curtains open. Unfortunately, when you were behind the screen your silhouette was clearly visible to the audience so l was greeted with the enthusiastic catcalls of 'Come on Haggar, put your back into it'.

No sooner had I returned to the operating box than the usherette contacted me on the intercom to inform me that the cinema was getting cold and would I come and stoke the boiler?

Now, the boiler happened to be inside the auditorium which required me to walk into the cinema with a wheelbarrow full of coke, throw open the furnace door and stoke the boiler with the film in progress. This was a noisy and disruptive process.

No sooner had I finished replenishing the furnace than a local doctor, who was sitting at the end of the row next to the boiler and possessed a loud and booming voice and a very sombre red complexion (so much so it seemed that his entire circulatory system consisted of the very best vintage port) shouted at me: "Haggar, I came to the cinema to be entertained, which I expected to come from watching the film not from you playing antics behind the screen and then showing me your backside as a local stoker".

This amused the audience greatly and I, embarrassed, crept out of the cinema dragging my wheelbarrow behind me.

Sex and the Cinema

IT WAS during the sixties that films started to have a more liberal theme and sex goddesses, such as Brigitte Bardot and Rita Hayworth, were beginning to appear.

The one film that epitomised this more than any other was Federico Fellini's masterpiece *La Dolce Vita*. This starred the incredibly beautiful and curvaceous Swedish actress Anita Ekberg with Marcello Mastroianni.

Ekberg 'sizzled' in this film, which shocked the cinemagoing audiences and stunned the film critics.

Haggars Cinema in the 1950s.

The film contained a very famous scene where Ekberg bathes drunkenly at night in Rome's Trevi Fountain, her wet clothes sticking to her sensual body. Needless to say, this film attracted large audiences composed of a disproportionate number of young men who often stayed to watch the second showing.

When the projector reached the notorious fountain scene, it began clattering loudly and vibrating merrily. This meant that the film was full of joins and I needed to concentrate very hard to ensure it didn't snap.

What had happened was, by the time the film had reached the distant outpost of Pembroke, various operators had chopped out a few frames of the film to show to their mates. This shortened the scene and made Ekberg look as though she was engaged in a Michael Jackson dance.

When the performance was complete that evening, whilst rewinding, I thought I had better check the joins in the film to make sure they were not about to snap in the next performance. I noticed one section had been replaced in the wrong order; it was only about four frames.

I deftly removed it with the intention of putting it back in its correct position but, when looking at it through the film viewer, I noticed it was part of the very famous fountain scene. I thought 'my puerile adolescent friends in school would love to see this', so I slipped it into my pocket.

Next day at school this caused a sensation with the young boys. We were at our English class making the most of the viewing opportunity, when our English teacher suddenly burst in. He was a man of differential temperament, most of it disagreeable, tetchy and denunciating towards his luckless pupils.

"What have you got there Haggar?" he roared.

"Nothing sir," was my weak reply.

"Well," he bellowed, "let me see your nothing" snatching the film from my hand.

"How do you see this?" he said.

"You have to hold it up against the light on the window sir" I foolishly said, believing my helpfulness would mitigate my inevitable punishment.

He immediately rushed into his study and did not appear for a few minutes; next he appeared with a red and excited face, and sped into the adjoining classroom where the history teacher was. Minutes passed then he eventually returned.

"Haggar," he said, "you're an absolute disgrace. Do one hundred lines."

"On what, Sir?" I said.

"Write that you mustn't take dirty films to school."

"You want me to write that, Sir?" I said mischievously.

He looked at me haughtily and said: "Just make it, 'I mustn't look at films in school' – and, by the way, I am going to confiscate this."

"But Sir," I protested, "I have to put it back into the film otherwise I will be in trouble."

He replied "That's your problem," and stalked off.

I never did get my film clip back but I was told, many years later, that there was a lot of embarrassed tittering going on in the staff room that day!

Education and entertainment don't mix

ONE time during my teenage years, as I was returning from school at the time when I was in the middle of sitting my 'O' Levels, my father stopped me (I had to pass the cinema to get home).

"Tony," he said "I'm not feeling well so could you do the show for me tonight?" adding "Mike (the operator) is on holiday and there is no helper in the operating box."

That night I sat in the box trying to revise for my geography exam the next day, which was difficult, as operating the film alone you were either feeding arc lights, rewinding film or loading fresh reels into the projector. I finally finished the performance around 11pm, and by the time I locked up and got to bed it was around midnight.

I awoke suddenly the next morning, realising I had overslept and I was sitting my geography exam that morning. I jumped on my bicycle and rushed to school, which was about two miles away, uphill all the way. I finally got to the exam, hot and sweaty, when it was half way through.

"Where on earth have you been?" said the invigilating master. "You had better get straight to it."

The termination bell rang sooner than I expected, and whilst collecting the papers the teacher said to me: "Haggar do you realise you have probably failed this exam and it is one of your best subjects?"

"I know I have sir," I said, "I only managed to complete three out of the five questions."

"What on earth do you think you were doing?" said the master clearly irritated.

"Just entertaining people," I replied.

He gave me a very quizzical look!

The Team

TO FINISH, I would just like to remember the team who were involved in providing cinematographic entertainment to the people of Pembroke.

They were my brothers, Roy and John, who shared many of these experiences; Herbert Uka and Mike Kucyj, our operators, who were also great friends; the 'Boys in the Box' I recall, Donald Kingdom, Graham Davies and the Carr brothers. My protector Nellie, the usherette and Brian Thomas (Ginger), who helped us on numerous occasions.

Finally there was my father who took great pride in his cinema and giving pleasure to local people. He always described himself as a 'Showman', following the family tradition.

He often quoted the motto, which he said came from our great grandfather William Haggar (I somehow suspect more probably a Hollywood musical): "Always make the audience, laugh, cry, and send them home happy."

I think perhaps we did.

The golden years – long queues outside the cinema for 'Good Time Girl'.

Above: Tony, Vicki and Roy at Tony's daughter's wedding.

Left: Haggars with Swiss Cottage
Restaurant in the bay window.

Chapter 13
The Ballroom

BESIDES modernising the cinema, my father restored the ballroom to something of its former glory. As previously described, the building was originally the Pembroke Assembly Rooms built for the local gentry in the 1860s as the venue for their social functions.

The room was magnificent, high and lofty with a Wedgwood style ceiling of ornate plasterwork in pale blue and white. There were elegant regency windows, baroque styling in gold leaf and massive ornate sweep doors for dramatic entrances. Chandelier-style lighting and soft wall-lights were installed and, at a later stage, a superb sprung dance floor was laid. It was by far the best venue for many miles around and, as a result, was used for many ostentatious occasions.

The restaurant, at the front of the upper level, was also renovated but it did not really come to life until the mid-1950s, when it was taken over by my brother Roy and his wife Maggie, who re-named it 'The Swiss Cottage Restaurant'.

They offered a full menu to their customers and also provided specialist catering for the many large functions and weddings that were held in the ballroom. Many local ladies assisted them; I remember in particular Renee James and Margaret Scone. Before Roy and Maggie, the catering suite was run for many years by Courtland Wise and his wife, Ilsa; after retiring from Haggars, Courtland ran his own taxi service.

A tea bar was installed in the wide corridor between the restaurant and the ballroom to cater for late night functions and this was run by Lily Clark and her daughter Shirley.

The ballroom and restaurant, in combination, provided an elite venue for weddings and grand occasions. These would include the Rotary Ball, the Mayor's Ball, the Young Farmers' Ball, the Hunt Ball and the Showman's Ball, which Dad put on after the Michaelmas Fair for the visiting showmen.

The ballroom would be specially prepared for such functions: the tables would be arranged around the perimeter of the dance floor, beautifully bedecked in their snow white table cloths, flowers and formal place settings complete with silver wine buckets. The ornate, softly lit ballroom provided a warm and magical setting for any such event.

The ballroom was also, of course, popular for birthday parties, fund raising events, drama and ballet shows, olde time dancing and many other social occasions.

The Dances

HAGGARS Ballroom was a favourite rendezvous for the young people of the town and many married couples could boast of having met at the Saturday night dance, done their courting in the back row of the cinema and attended their wedding reception in the ballroom.

When there was a special occasion dance, Dad would take John, Tony and myself upstairs to the ballroom and give us a big bag of balloons to blow up.

We blew until our ears ached but thought it was great fun, especially when the prize might be a big bag of sweets or an ice cream.

Anyone who remembers those dances at Haggars will remember that magical moment when the balloon net was released and the balloons floated down on the dancers. Couples had to 'dance wide' until the balloons between them burst.

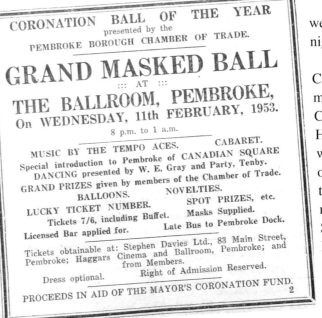

CORONATION BALL OF THE YEAR
presented by the
PEMBROKE BOROUGH CHAMBER OF TRADE.

GRAND MASKED BALL
::: AT :::
THE BALLROOM, PEMBROKE,
On WEDNESDAY, 11th FEBRUARY, 1953.
8 p.m. to 1 a.m.

MUSIC BY THE TEMPO ACES.   CABARET.
Special introduction to Pembroke of CANADIAN SQUARE DANCING presented by W. E. Gray and Party, Tenby.
GRAND PRIZES given by members of the Chamber of Trade.
BALLOONS.   NOVELTIES.
LUCKY TICKET NUMBER.   SPOT PRIZES, etc.
Tickets 7/6, including Buffet.   Masks Supplied.
Licensed Bar applied for.   Late Bus to Pembroke Dock.

Tickets obtainable at: Stephen Davies Ltd., 83 Main Street, Pembroke; Haggars Cinema and Ballroom, Pembroke; and from Members.
Dress optional.   Right of Admission Reserved.
PROCEEDS IN AID OF THE MAYOR'S CORONATION FUND. 2

The highlights of the week were the Thursday and Saturday night dances.

In the 1950s the name Charlie Bumstead was synonymous with Haggars Ballroom. Charlie, who originated from Hastings, enlisted in the Army when he was just sixteen years old and, after training, joined the Royal Hussars. His love of music led to him to the Army School of Music at Kneller Hall, Middlesex, where he trained with Norman Wisdom: Charlie taught him to play the drums.

Charlie was a very versatile musician, proficient as a saxophonist, clarinettist and flautist. His last posting was Merrion Camp, after which he settled locally and formed the Tempo Aces dance band.

He recruited talented musicians Dickie Luff and Jimmy Viggars (trumpet), Danny Hordley, Levi Williams and Ken Moody (piano accordion), Iris Brickle (piano) and various drummers as time went by. The first drummer was Cliff Lloyd followed by Norman Wren, Tommy Mills, Charlie Allen and Dennis Williams.

ROYAL AIR FORCES
ASSOCIATION
Incorporated by Royal
Charter.
Registered under War
Charities Act 1940.
THE ANNIVERSARY
BATTLE OF BRITAIN BALL
in THE BALLROOM, PEMBROKE,
on Friday, 18th September.
Dancing 8 to 1. Spot and other Prizes.
M.C.: Mr. W. Neil. Tempo Aces Band.
Tickets : 3/- obtainable from
Haggar's Cinema and other sellers or
R.A.F.A. Club. Admission will be
strictly controlled by ticket. Bus to
Pembroke Dock. (1-18-9)

Battle of Britain Ball at Haggars Ballroom.

Anyone who went to the pictures on a Saturday night could always tell when the dance started up: overhead there was a muffled thumping sound: the drums in Charlie's band! Even the expensive sprung floor did not baffle the sound of Charlie and his entourage giving it 'whoopee' upstairs. It was all part of the show at Haggars!

Superintendent J. Jones, the Police Chief stationed at Pembroke Dock, used to love going to Haggars Cinema. The last film show on a Thursday night, a dance night, was usually his venue if off duty.

If the band in the ballroom overhead played a very lively number and the footfall upstairs started to resound in the cinema below, he would send a message upstairs asking that the band played something 'a little less rousing'.

Vernon Scott wrote a series for the *Western Telegraph* called 'Just a Thought' and thanks to him we have some amusing anecdotes about Charlie Bumstead and the Tempo Aces in our old ballroom.

No-one has more vivid memories of evenings in Haggars Ballroom, Pembroke than the musicians who played there. From their elevated positions on stage they looked down on

Charlie Bumstead's Tempo Aces at Haggars. The line-up includes Norman Wren on drums, Iris Brickle on piano, Danny Hordley on piano accordian and Charlie himself on saxophone.

couples gliding past with arms entwined, as the rotating crystal ball attached to the ceiling and illuminated by spot lights spun pretty, coloured patterns around the room.

It wasn't all smooch stuff, however. When Charlie Bumstead's Tempo Aces belted out the 'Woodchoppers' Ball' and suchlike, the jitterbuggers came into their own!

A space either side of the platform was favoured by these fast twirling, arm-twisting, knee-bending, inter-changing athletic types, and one night in the 1950s the unbelievable happened – part of the floor collapsed because of their uninhibited exertions!

Dancers screamed, shrieked and shouted with horror, firmly believing they were about to free-fall into the cinema below and end up straddled across the one and nines.

Tempo Aces' drummer Dennis Williams takes up the story: 'For a while there was pandemonium, but fortunately the floor was balanced on three inch springs and it was for that measurement only it gave way! For those involved it was a frightening experience, but it certainly did not put them off jitterbugging'.

When the band chose Latin American numbers, there were always volunteers to play the maracas. Two young local Red Cross workers, Brenda Morris and Marion Hay, were fond of helping out, as was Cardiff policeman and Welsh rugby international Mike Knill, a Pembroke boy who patronised Haggars in the 1950s when home on leave.

Charlie's daughter, Pam Ball, recalls that her father always insisted that the band play Home on the Range for the last dance:

Oh give me a home where the buffalo roam, where the deer and the antelope play. Where seldom is heard a discouraging word and the sky is not cloudy all day.

Then came the chorus:

Home, home on the range, where the deer and the antelope play. Where seldom is heard a discouraging word, and the skies are not cloudy all day.

Band members tried, unsuccessfully to persuade Charlie to play something more romantic, but he wouldn't budge.

As Iris Brickle (pianist of the band) put it: "Who wanted to share a home with a buffalo?"

The last dance was always preceded, incidentally, by a much more pacey number, The Sheik of Araby.

at 7.30 p.m.   (D789

SPECIAL ANNOUNCEMENT:
ROCK AND ROLL
REVIVAL HITS PEMBROKESHIRE
Don't miss the SENSATIONAL
FORGOTTEN FIVE SHOW BAND
AT
HAGGAR'S BALLROOM, Pembroke
THIS SATURDAY
ADMISSION 7/6.   DANCING 8 - 11.45 p.m.
                                (D790

The New Palladium Ballroom
PEMBROKE DOCK. Telephone: Pembroke 2636

Haggars Ballroom in the late 1950s. Len Haggar is kneeling on the right of the picture with Pam on his left.

In another article, Vernon Scott interviewed Iris Brickle, when she was aged 90.

Iris had accepted an invitation to join the newly formed Tempo Aces in the late 1940s. She recalled that, while dances elsewhere in Pembrokeshire were free of violence, trouble did occasionally flare-up at Haggars during the summer months because so many reserve soldiers, training at Castlemartin, attended dances there. This kept the bouncers busy, earning their pay packets the hard way.

DENNIS Williams remembers an evening in 1956 when a full scale fight broke out at Haggars involving uniformed Z Men, as Army reservist were known at the time.

"We couldn't have left that night even if we'd wanted to," Dennis recalled. "An Army sergeant ordered the band to carry on playing and stood guard at the front of the stage. Amid all the mayhem we were playing numbers like *The Tennessee Waltz* and *I'll See You in my Dreams*!

I remember Timmy Jones puffing and panting as he passed us holding a Z Man in a headlock. The chap was purple in the face and I shouted 'Relax your hold, he can't breathe!' Timmy shouted back, 'if he can't breathe, he can't fight!'

A police officer, Derek Davies, who was from Llangwm, entered the ballroom and within seconds some of the reservists were playing rugby with his helmet! It was that sort of an evening!"

It should be emphasised that dances at Haggars were near-

Police v soldiers in the Ballroom.

"PITCHED BATTLE" IN DANCE HALL

POLICE HURT AT PEMBROKE

"Military Should Be Ashamed"

"Three or four civilian policemen cannot cope with an insurrection," commented Ald. W. J. Gwilliam (Chairman) at a special Pembroke Court on Tuesday when announcing the decision in a case in which four London Territorials were stated to have behaved in a local dance hall in a manner which was a disgrace to the British Army.

Before the court were Rifleman David Way (21), James Robert Barrs ?, James Hill (20), of the Queen's Westminster Rifles and Trooper

"EVERYBODY WAS FIGHTING."

Ronald John Thomas, 19, St. Anne's Crescent, Pembroke, stated that when he went into the dance "everybody was fighting." He saw the two P.C. Davieses there. "I saw P.C. (71) Davies stop a man hit a woman and the next I saw he was on the floor," witness added. "I saw Barrs and Hill on P.C. Davies and Way and Frost kicking at him." Later he was in the Main Street and was asked by P.S. Morgan to identify the men as they were coming out of the bus.

A BLOODSTAINED BELT.

P.S. Morgan informed the court that at Pembroke railway station when the four men were being taken to Swansea, he saw the blood-stained belt (produced) around Barr. On his instructions the belt was removed. He was present when the last witness identified the defendants as they got off the bus.

FLYING BOTTLES AND CHAIRS.

L/Cpl. G. Lawton, R.M.P., said he was on duty in Pembroke, and entered the Ballroom at the same time as P.C. (71) Davies, the other constable following. "There was fighting all over the Ballroom and bottles and chairs were thrown at us to try to stop us," he declared. "I saw P.C. (71) Davies slip and Frost kick him on the left side of the face. Frost struck me in the eye and blackened it and I had to receive medical attention. I saw other

ly always enjoyable and orderly occasions, and there was seldom trouble with regular troops stationed at Llanion Barracks, Pembroke Dock, or the R.A.F. from the local flying boat base.

But, as Dennis Williams said: "Come the summer and the arrival of the Reserve Army regiments, things could get very lively indeed."

In 1961 another force arrived in Pembroke to swell the numbers in our dances and provide competition for the local boys. This was the German Panzer division which was posted to Merrion camp and created national news with many protesters converging on Pembroke to strongly object to their presence.

There were umpteen anti-German demonstrations and the town was flooded with press; in particular the Tabloids who were looking for sensational news and created no end of trouble.

The German soldiers, however, like any other young men, wanted to enjoy themselves and naturally went to the Saturday night dances.

The girls were swept off their feet by the bowing, heel clicking and courtesy when they were hand chaperoned on to the floor and back to their seats. This was a little disturbing for the local boys, but it all seemed to work and the dances continued with reasonably civilized behaviour.

The swinging sixties

CHARLIE passed away in the spring of 1964 after a long illness, a very sad loss but fondly remembered by the many couples who first met at the dances.

This really marked the end of the era of the post war ballroom dances: tastes and expectations of people were about to change dramatically as a new generation ushered in the swinging sixties.

My brother Tony, who was very much on the ball and persuaded dad to adapt to the changing scene, continues the story.

THIS was the time of my brother John and my youth, it was 'our generation' and we wanted to be part of what was happening. The attendances at the Saturday dance were falling dramatically and change was being demanded.

I was determined to be part of this new era. With a few friends we started practising (badly) the new emerging music but, as a result, we started to understand and appreciate the huge variety of music and talent that was emerging.

My school friends were beginning to collect the new American music: Dylan had taken Nashville by storm and the likes of Elvis and Chuck Berry were becoming major influences on the teenagers of the day. Suddenly the Mersey Sound was rapidly emerging and my brother John and I felt we had to be part of this and provide it for our local audiences.

Cheekily John and I told my father that, if we started to book rock and other groups to try out on a Thursday night, we thought we could considerably change our business fortunes. I was given the 'go ahead' and soon discovered an intense and talented music scene in the Swansea valley.

The interest in this new music was far more than I had imagined and I knew we needed to bring it to West Wales. I met as many of these new groups as I could find and amassed a list of contacts from the music shops, which was to prove invaluable.

In addition there were a number of demo disc companies emerging in Swansea who were only too keen for us to hear their collections.

Immediately we started hiring these new bands, all of which were keen to make their name in the music world. They would often arrive at the ballroom in a second-hand ambulance or some such vehicle that had been cheaply procured.

The new rock music was an immediate success, and the enthusiasm of the young people was overwhelming. Suddenly the dances were highly successful and more was demanded: there was great excitement in being present and seeing this new music scene unfold.

Many of those early groups that visited the ballroom went on to become well known musicians in the rock world and with a variety of successes. Some names spring to mind. The Eyes of Blue (from Neath), whose lead guitar Taff Williams and bass man Ritchie Francis were outstandingly talented players with superb vocal harmonies (in 1966, the band won the Melody Maker Beat Contest and signed for Decca's Dream label).

Another great group was the Corncrackers (from Llanelli) who had unique harmonies and worked with many of the big groups; they played support to acts such as Johnny Kidd & the Pirates and The Hollies.

The other outstanding South Wales groups I recall were notably, The Blackjacks and Peter Shane & the Vikings, but there were many, many others. We got to know these groups reasonably well and many of them became good friends.

The '60s remembered

RAY Dony, whose group The Valiants used to play in the ballroom in the 'Swinging Sixties', remembers Saturday night dances at Haggars:

Terry Duignan and I decided to form a group. We both knew a few chords on the guitar so with Dave Gledhill on drums and Bryan (Benny) John singing, we approached John Haggar to play in the interval at the Saturday night dances.

After a few months Ray Reynolds took over on the drums.

In those days, the early sixties, the resident band was run by Charlie Bumstead, with Denis Williams on drums, a lady piano player, and a few brass and woodwind players.

The bouncers were Timmy Jones, a chap called Otto and a chap called Ball. Lily Clark and her daughter Pamela ran the tea bar, as there was no alcohol sold. Brian (Ginger) Thomas took the entrance fee – 3/6.

When the Panzers came to Castlemartin, a German film crew came to Haggars to film the Panzers being taught to jive by the local girls.

In addition to the 'Swansea Sound' a number of local groups were forming: the ones I recall were The Valiants, formed by Terry Duignan with Ray Dony, Benny John and Ray Reynolds and Don Wade and The Wayfarers from Milford Haven, all of whom were popular with our audiences.

On numerous occasions we actually booked groups who had made their names in the rock world. I recall The Mindbenders from Manchester, who had a hit with *A Groovy Kind of Love*, The Merseybeats and Screaming Lord Sutch, who for some bizarre reason became quite popular and is mostly remembered standing for lost hopes as a parliamentary candidate.

This all sounds very grand, but at that time the music business was a tough, demanding, and unpredictable business. The traditional music moguls had lost their influence and the new musical talents coming to the forefront did so as a result of their popularity with young people.

The Iveys were regulars at Haggars in The Swinging Sixties.

Often, when dealing with a large London booking agency to get a well known band, the negotiations could only be described as 'very interesting!'

These often unscrupulous agents would demand ludicrous prices on a first enquiry but within 10 minutes you could usually reach a deal at around 20% of the asking price; little did they know they were dealing with a spotty seventeen year old at the other end of the telephone who, in law, had no right to make a binding legal contract! Another complication was that the booking agents were not the personal agents of the band, which led to a further raft of negotiations.

Partly due to this plethora of middle men, the groups often got a very bad deal. On numerous occasions at the end of a gig, we would be approached by the band for a sub.

There were a number of regrets, occasions when we came close to but did not secure bookings with some very notable bands: we all would have cherished the opportunity to see some of the now rock icons at their best. The ones that come to mind are The Kinks and the Beatles.

The Kinks (after a long and arduous set of negotiations) were booked and a date set but, on the night of the gig, just one hour before the performance, we received a telegram and sick note that they were not arriving.

I actually, to my great excitement, secured a booking for the Beatles but, unfortunately for us, they had their first hit *Love Me Do* in 1962, just a couple of weeks before their gig. All existing deals were cancelled as a result. Luckily the publicity for the gig had not gone out, which really would have disappointed our customers.

To gain entry, one really had to be on one's best behaviour and there were three doormen who made sure that no one loutish or highly inebriated gained admittance.

Timmy Jones was a burly insurance agent with the Prudential; Otto Muller, a giant of a man, was a former German paratrooper while Norman Hughes had earned his reputation of being a tough guy fighting in Taylor's boxing booth at the fair.

The bouncers – Otto Muller, Timmy Jones and Norman Hughes.

Any trouble whilst getting past those three and – 'mind your manners' – down the stairs you went.

We also had our MC, Brian Thomas (Ginger). Brian would assist in a number of ways: announcing the dances, 'calling' at a traditional dance and generally assisting. He was also a reasonable crooner and enjoyed nothing more than to accompany the dance band with a favourite song.

Other members of staff included our cloakroom attendants; for the men, Tommy Griffiths and for the ladies, Mrs. Morris. These were jobs that required great efficiency for, at the end of a dance, there would be a mass of people clamouring for their coats at the same time, all hurrying to catch the last bus home.

In the 1950s stiletto heels were all the fashion and one of Mrs. Morris's jobs was to hand out plastic heel clips which fitted over the stilettos to prevent them gouging the precious sprung floor. Despite her best efforts, the clips were not a great success and the stilettos caused so much damage that eventually the floor had to be replaced.

In my early twenties, I decided that I had had my fill of the entertainment business and decided that I would move on.

The business was hard and demanding and my brother John and I were not only involved in running the cinema and dances, but we also had full time jobs.

I was in the final stages of professional exams and was looking elsewhere for a long term future. John decided to enter the family business, which by then was too much for our ageing father.

The dancing gigs were slowly drawing to a close as groups became mega stars with enormous and elaborate concerts. They continued for a few years more but, as always in the entertainment business, change was on its way. Local cinemas and dances were severely hit by the popularity of the growing interest in television and finally ended in the eighties at Haggars.

However, Haggars was adapting to change, as we shall see in the next chapter.

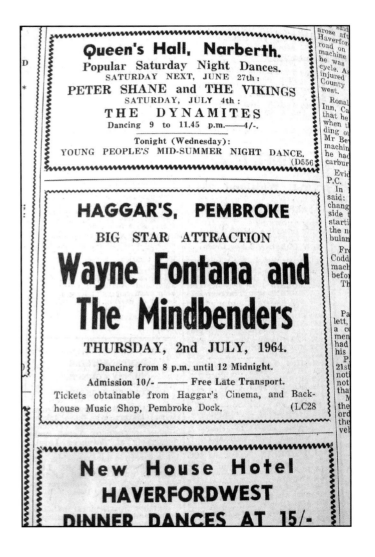

Chapter 14
The Final Curtain

WITH the passing of time, public tastes changed and the advent of television was eroding cinema audiences; needless to say, the Haggar children must have been the last in Pembroke to have a television.

Our mum, Pam went out and bought one in the end as Dad would not even have the word 'television' mentioned in the house; the air was blue in the Haggar household for some considerable time after that!

However, my father had not yet finished building his empire. The building which once housed the Palace Cinema in Queen's Street, Pembroke Dock, came on the market in the late 1970s and Dad saw this as an opportunity to expand his cinema business.

The building has an interesting history stretching back to around 1904, when it was built as the Queen's Theatre by Walter Canton. It was taken over in 1908 by Tom Barger at a time, incidentally, when William Haggar set up a temporary show on land at Hawkestone Road.

In 1910 the Palace again changed hands and, under the ownership of Sidney 'Daddy' White, became White's Picture Palace showing silent movies together with live vaudeville acts.

This lasted until 1914 when the Palace returned to the Barger family; Martha Lyon Barger, widow of Tom, took it on again with her two sons and renamed it Barger's Palace.

They later undertook a complete refurbishment of the building and reopened it in December 1920 as the New Palace Cinema.

However, in 1930 it closed for good: competition from a new purpose-built cinema, The Grand, coupled with the depression resulting from the closure of the dockyard led to its demise and, for the following 50 years, it was used as a furniture warehouse.

L. W. Haggar and Sons spent £50,000 purchasing and renovating the property, which was run by my brother John who was, at that time, taking a leading role in the business.

New projection equipment was fitted and the seating area re-vamped to provide 430 seats; the Palace was now considerably larger than the Pembroke Cinema and it re-opened under the wing of Haggars in 1980.

It opened with a showing of *Alien* but audiences were decreasing and the Palace, after only a few years of its cinema revival, was to become a bingo hall. This was managed by Jim Dyer, a member of the family who really loved his bingo and proved to be a very popular and successful manager.

The Astoria in Milford Haven, the Pavilion in Cardigan and the Warren in Tenby (the former auction rooms) were also run by John during this period; the Astoria and the Warren as bingo halls and the Pavilion as a cinema, bingo hall and snooker club.

Bingo in the ballroom, 1973.

WESTERN TELEGRAPH, Wednesday, February 29th, 1984

Last picture show soon as cinema prepares for snooker

BY VERNON SCOTT

Once upon a time long queues ming outside for admission to gar's Cinema, Pembroke, e a common enough sight. ut now there is a strong possi-y that cues of a different kind be found inside the old cine- for the owners want to con- it into a snooker club!

s week managing director Haggar confirmed that pro- g the necessary planning con- s forthcoming from South rokeshire District Council. inema will cease to function conversion work will get way for the snooker hall t.

that happens the Haggar s long association with the a in Pembroke, stretching me 70 years, will come to

William, had owned it before him. The cinema building, in the mid- dle of the Castle Town's Main Street, was once known as the Pembroke Assembly Rooms and was much favoured by officers of the local yeomanry.

When it changed hands a cine- ma screen was erected there by a man named Phillips, to show the pioneering silent 'flicks' made popular during the first world war.

At that time, and earlier in the century, the Haggars were well known South Wales showmen whose primitive movies and magic lantern displays drew thousands of goggle-eyed locals to country fairs.

There will be considerable irony in the fact that if John Haggar does close the Pembroke cinema, it will not be through lack of public support, although this of course, is

biggest bugbear of all is VAT. We are believed to be the last of the small town cinemas in the British Isles, and a lot of heart searching took place before we decided that enough was enough.

"We shall be submitting a change of use planning application for consideration by the District Council's planning committee in late March, and if they agree to the cinema becoming a snooker hall for club members, then we shall go ahead. If the application is refused then I still cannot say for certain that the cinema will remain open."

In recent years Haggar's have expanded their business substan- tially, taking over the old Astoria Cinema at Milford Haven, the Pavilion at Cardigan, as well as reopening the Palace at Pembroke Dock.

that pictures of the right quality, especially films suitable for all the family, will still pull the crowds in. But the trouble is that for every film like that available, we have to book others with much less appeal," he points out.

It is all a far cry from the era when the name Haggar always spelt family entertainment at the cinema, and huge crowds queued regularly to watch their heroes — and heroines — of the silver screen.

The odds are that John Haggar will be remembered as "The last of the cinema Haggars" — and for people with long memories that will be very sad indeed.

● See this week's Then And Now on page 19.

Closing soon: Cinema owner John Haggar outside Haggar's Cinema in Pembroke whi wants to convert into a snooker club. (Telegraph pict

Bingo had already been introduced into the Ballroom at Haggars in 1973, although dances, discos and events continued to be held there.

John managed events when Dad's health was deteriorating, and, on his death, was destined to inherit the business. My father found it very difficult to admit that the time had come to vacate his seat at Haggars; show-business was his life.

However, he kept in touch by regularly visiting the bingo, sitting at the back in 'Mr Haggar's designated seat' chatting, joking and enjoying the atmosphere. He was often seen sitting on a stool next to Irene Lloyd, the Ballroom cashier, chatting and 'doing his bit' by tearing the entrance tickets for the bingo.

Due to my father's determination, Haggars of Pembroke lasted longer than most, the family having treasured the silver screen for almost 90 years. Changing times and market forces, however, eventually led to the closure of the cinema in 1984.

It is a blessing that my father did not live to see the demise of his beloved cinema for Leonard Walter Haggar passed away at home in June 1981.

Despite television and video, Haggars could still draw in the crowds. However, by the beginning of 1984 John was con- sidering closing the cinema even though, at the time, scores of people had been turned away for the showing of *Jungle Book* and the new James Bond movie had played to full houses.

In an interview by Vernon Scott, published in the *West Wales Telegraph* dated 29th February 1984, John explained:

VAT coupled with increasing overheads and decreasing revenue has forced us to seriously consider closing the cinema. The biggest bugbear of all is VAT. We are believed to be the last of the small town cinemas in the British Isles, and a lot of heart-searching took place before we decided that enough was enough.

We have proved in Pembroke that pictures of the right quality, especially films suitable for all the family, will still pull the crowds in. But the trouble is that for every film like that available, we have to book others with much less appeal.

We shall be submitting a change of use planning application for consideration by the District Council's planning committee in late March and, if they agree to the cinema becoming a snooker hall for club members, then we shall go ahead.

Vernon Scott commented: "The odds are that John Haggar will be remembered as the last of the cinema Haggars – and for people with long memories that will be very sad indeed."

IN MAY 1984, planning permission for the snooker hall having been granted, Haggars Cinema showed its last film.

One of the last young men to work in the cinema operating box was a local lad called Jonathon James and my youngest son, Danny Dyer also assisted after school and at weekends.

He remembers the last film ever to be shown in the Cinema was *Young Frankenstein*, a popular 1974 American comedy horror film directed by Mel Brooks and starring Gene Wilder. I must not forget to mention that the record for ice-cream sales from the tray was held by Danny, who took sixty pounds selling Strawberry Mivvi's and King Cones during the excitement of *Superman 3*.

Following that final show, the cinema was converted into a snooker hall. John's right-hand-man was his brother-in-law Ron Rees, husband of Sue, while Len's eldest grandson Philip Cheverton helped to build and design the snooker hall before becoming its manager.

Ron, Philip, Fred Lloyd and Brian Williams worked long and hard to convert the premises and snooker, growing in popularity, was soon a favourite feature at Haggars. Ron Rees opened a very popular toy and gift shop where the cinema entrance once was, extending the frontage and levelling the floor: it was run by Fred's wife, Irene, who also acted as cashier for the bingo hall.

In January 1986 the Ballroom was transformed into a fitness centre. A report in the *Western Telegraph* by Jackie Denning declared:

The ballroom at Haggar's Cinema in Pembroke's Main Street has been transformed into the main hall of the Pembroke Health and Fitness Centre, which opened recently.

And the highly polished, highly professional looking room is the result of many weeks of hard work by husband and wife, Phil and Alyson Nicholas, and Phil Cheverton whose grandmother Mrs Pam Haggar owns the building.

With the help of 'A' Level art student Michelle Sucksmith, who decided on the colour scheme and made all the blinds, curtains and upholstery, the three health and fitness enthusiasts have created a unique leisure complex offering a range of classes and activities – since it was opened, the centre has become a popular meeting place and visitors are encouraged to stay for the day to savour the delights of the fruit bar, where a health food lunch prepared by Alyson is currently served on Thursdays.

A dance and fitness instructor, Alyson is very pleased with the new venture, 'The response we have had has been marvellous and it shows that there is a need in Pembroke for this sort of amenity', she said.

Almost as a tribute to the magnificent Ballroom, which forms the centrepiece of the new complex, the team hopes to have ballroom dancing – another class to add to the ever-increasing list at what must be one of the area's most popular new leisure centres.

DESPITE all the changes, however, it was not to last. First, the snooker hall closed and became Paddles Night Club.

Worse was to follow. In 1992 the beautiful Ballroom with its Victorian architraves was stripped of its grandeur and converted into flats: my brother Roy tried in vain to get the Ballroom listed in order to stop this travesty, but to no avail.

However, before that happened, there was one last performance.

The East End Flyover Company had made use of the Ballroom for a short time to prepare scenery for drama productions which were held in various premises in the area such as the Stackpole Centre, St Mary's Church and, on one memorable occasion, Haggars Ballroom itself.

The last known photograph of the Ballroom.

The set for the last show at Haggars, 'A Penny for a Song' presented by 'The East End Flyover Company'.

Their production in 1992 of *A Penny for a Song* with a cast of thirteen and a set designed by Warren Heaton was the last time a public performance was held in this lovely building.

The amazing scenery and backcloths were designed and painted by George and Jeanne Lewis using the Ballroom floor as an artist's easel.

George told me about the time when he was painting a backcloth for that last production and the paint went through the cloth onto the Ballroom floor. George was very concerned, as he knew how precious this floor had been to Len. He passed his concern on to Ron Rees who said: "Don't worry George – it's all coming down in a few weeks."

What a tragic loss to Pembroke! It was the end of an era.

A scene from the last show at Haggars, 'A Penny for a Song' presented by local drama group 'The East End Flyover Company'.

THE CINEMA is now a nightclub: there are no more cuddles in the back row, no hanging baskets and flower tubs on the front canopy, no-one dressed in a suit and dickey bow to smile and tilt his hat to the ladies or acknowledge the gents by saying, "How are you doing boss?"

It was never the cinema to Dad but always 'The Show'.

Barbara Cook remarked in a letter she wrote to the local paper headed 'Sorry about the fate of Haggars': *Thanks Haggars for my special and now sad memories. You certainly deserve better than becoming flats.*

Sadly, the phrase 'the show must go on' will never apply to Haggars again.

The social loss to the town coupled with the loss to the entertainment industry, was a hard blow to bear. Sadly, not only the loss of the last remaining Haggars Cinema but also the end of a family tradition.

Goodnight Haggars.

PART THREE
Haggar Remembered
A remarkable legacy

Chapter 15
Uncovering the History

IOWE much of what I know about my great grandfather to my late brother Roy Haggar, who was the family historian.

Although William Haggar is now acknowledged as a pioneer of the British Film industry, this was not always the case: Roy felt very strongly that he had not been given the recognition due to him and did much to bring about public recognition of our great grandfather's work.

The early British film industry had very much been lost in time – its origins unacknowledged. However, in 1946, the British Film Institute (or National Film Library as it was called then) commissioned Roger Manvell and Rachael Low to write *The History of the British Film: 1896-1946* to commemorate the first fifty years of the cinema in Britain.

For the fiftieth anniversary, a compilation of the silent films held in the BFI's archive was shown in cinemas and it was fortunate that this was seen by William Haggar's youngest daughter, Lily Richards.

In that compilation of films she saw a Haggar film which had apparently been lost: *The Life of Charles Peace* in which she had acted along with her brothers Walter and Jim and sister Violet. The film, which is about the notorious Victorian burglar and murderer who was hanged for the murder of Arthur Dyson, was shot in and around Pembroke Dock and had been wrongly attributed to Frank Mottershaw, who had also made a film about Peace.

Lily contacted the BFI to put matters right, just in time for it to be included in Low and Manvell's first volume of *The History of the British Film* published in 1948.

This was an exciting discovery as the bulk of William Haggar's films had been lost. *The Life of Charles Peace* is one of the oldest extant British story films and enabled a true appraisal of the importance of William Haggar's work for, until its discovery, only *A Desperate Poaching Affray* plus fragments were recognised as Haggar films.

Had it not been for Lily's chance viewing of the film, this would not have happened.

She further highlighted her father's life and work in interviews and, towards the end of her life, she dictated her biography to her daughter, June Bilous: this has never been published.

Another discovery was made years later and this was largely due to a BBC Radio Wales documentary in June 1984 entitled *Haggar's Travelling Picture Show* in which Roy Haggar took part. Phyllis Haggar happened to hear the broadcast – and she also happened to have a film stored in the cupboard under the stairs of her Swansea home.

This turned out to be *The Maid of Cefn Ydfa* which had been passed between different members of the Haggar family, eventually ending up in her home where it had lain for many years.

The film was in three reels which were disintegrating in their cans, stored in a galvanised lined box. Phyllis gave it to the BFI for restoration and fortunately, although the final scene is missing, we are now able to enjoy 38 minutes of the orginal 50 minute film.

This was not the original *Maid of Cefn Ydfa* of 1902, one of the first fictional films ever produced and which literally made William's fortune that momentous night when it was first shown at Treorchy fair. The film was a later, longer, remake produced by Will Haggar Jnr., who starred in it with his wife Jenny Lindon playing the star crossed lovers, Will Hopcyn and Ann Thomas.

Celebrating the Haggar film legacy in Pembroke Town Hall.

Will had hired a professional cameraman and turned to his father for editing. William Haggar did not approve of what he saw – so much so that he insisted on re-shooting many scenes and spent a great deal of time editing the rest. It was released in 1914.

Fortunately, my grandfather Walter wrote his memoirs. His memories of the travelling theatre years were published in *Dock Leaves* in 1955, but his fascinating account of the 'Travelling Bioscope Show', written later, remained unpublished until now – I am pleased that at last it can be read in full.

This memoir is a first hand account of the birth of the cinema in Wales and as such is an invaluable resource to everyone interested in cinema history.

As previously stated, William Haggar's contribution to the development of moving pictures had been forgotten and Roy, who was close to Walter, was inspired by him to take up the cause, to ensure that William Haggar's true place in cinema history be properly recognised.

He became the family historian, writing, lecturing and giving interviews. In 1988, he was consulted by BBC Wales for a film they were making about the life of William Haggar, a film which led to an awakening of national interest in the film pioneer. It was called *A Penny for your Dreams – I Fro Breuddwydion* in the Welsh language version which, translates as *Into the Vale of Dreams*.

The film was a dramatised biography, the story of a remarkable man who trailed his family around the country with his travelling theatre, gambled everything on his conviction that the future was in moving pictures and became, himself, a successful film director. Ken Howard directed the film and William and Sarah Haggar were played by Dafydd Hywel and Sue Roderick.

In the wake of the success of the film, there was a major exhibition at the Welsh Folk Museum, St Fagan's – headlined in the *South Wales Echo* 1988 as 'Honour at last for film pioneer'.

BBC Arts website comments thus: *Fortunately, at last, people are aware of what William Haggar meant to British film making having spectacularly made around 60 films, 34 of them documented. They reveal an extraordinarily, progressive grasp of editing and screen framing techniques and an ability to stage action of rare gusto, drawing partly on his blood and thunder stage melodramas.*

IT WAS particularly gratifying to Roy that William Haggar's true place in cinema history had been recognised.

Possessing a great talent and a true pioneering spirit, William courageously pursued his dreams and convictions in the face of great adversity and was always looking to improve and innovate. He invented the panning shot, something we take for granted today. In those early days, pictures were shot as if the actors were on a stage in front of a stationary camera; Haggar followed the actors with his camera, – something no one had done before.

He also invented something which is very much with us today – the chase sequence. Haggar did it first in his *A Desperate Poaching Affray* 1903 (also known as *The Poachers*) which was Gaumont's most popular British film with around 480 copies sold, not only at home but in America, and is accredited as the forerunner of the Keystone Cops.

He is also attributed as being the originator of the 'series': a sequence of very short comedies one of the most popular featuring 'Mirthful Mary', a boozy heroine who would engage in a knock for knock with the police and anyone else in authority.

National Library Wales in Aberystwyth, home of the National Screen and Sound Archive of Wales.

This might be irreverent, but then William Haggar was very much a man of the people and, in sending up authority figures for a laugh, he was appealing very much to popular humour.

Another series was that of the exploits of 'Weary Willie and Tired Tim', two accident-prone tramps.

IN 2000, another fortunate discovery was made. This was *The Sheep Stealer* which had formed part of the Abbé Joye's private collection in Switzerland and was acquired by the British Film Institute.

'Pioneer's long-lost film discovered' announced the *Western Telegraph* on 26th January and reported the efforts made by archivists and film historians to research the film's origins.

This prompted my brother Roy to comment: *I wrote to both the National Film Archive and the Wales Archive long before the discovery of this latest film offering my help with any they didn't recognise and I'm amazed that they haven't referred it to me.*

After all, I remember many of the actors from my childhood, and William Haggar never made a film without the family, so I'm one of the few people who can recognise them with absolute certainty.

Seven years later, another film *Revenge*, filmed in 1904, was found in the U.S. Library of Congress, where a copy was deposited to claim copyright. Who knows, there may be more Haggar films out there waiting to be found?

Strictly speaking of course, my great grandfather was English. But he thought of Wales as his home; it was where he entertained the crowds with his travelling bioscope and where he made all his films. Wales took him to its heart and claimed him as its own.

A few years ago I visited the National Library Wales at Aberystwyth to find out more about William Haggar. The National Library houses the National Screen and Sound Archive of Wales which aims to preserve, promote and celebrate the sound and moving image heritage of Wales.

The Archive is home to a comprehensive collection of films, television programmes, videos, sound and music recordings relating to Wales and the Welsh. It was established in 2001, when the Wales Film and Television Archive was merged with the National Library of Wales' Sound and Moving Image Collection and is funded by the NLW and the Welsh government.

I was delighted to discover that great pride is taken in the Haggar connection. There is a Haggar Room and I was shown a 1905, 35mm silent film projector which was believed to have been used by William Haggar himself. I was also given a copy of a photograph of William Haggar and family – a still taken from one of the films *A Stepney Wedding*, which I had not previously seen.

A fine painting of my grandfather Walter is also displayed there, although not as I remember him. The posed picture of him immaculately dressed in a suit (see page 84) is a far cry from the casually dressed, relaxed and easy going grandpa the family all knew and loved!

Vicki with Jon Reed, Film Preservation Officer, NLW Aberystwyth, and William Haggar's silent film projector

In Pembroke, the name Haggar is remembered with great affection. So many Pembroke people have fond memories of Haggars: going to the pictures in the cinema as well as dances and events in the ballroom. Its loss is still much regretted.

In his lifetime, Roy did so much to keep alive the memory of his great grandfather and inspired his daughter Sarah to continue the tradition. As the fifth Haggar generation, Sarah is an actress, a teacher of drama and has produced several plays at the Torch Theatre.

It was just before his death in 2009, that Roy recorded a digital story, or short film, about the Haggar family for a project of Pembroke & Monkton Local History Society entitled *Through my Eyes: a Community History of Pembroke and Monkton.*

This project, devised and led by Linda and Stuart Asman, traces the history of Pembroke through the stories of local people and has been published as a DVD and accompanying book. I also became involved, making my own digital story entitled 'Growing up in Main Street'.

My association with the Pembroke & Monkton Local Society gave me the impetus to do everything I could to keep the memory of Haggars alive in Pembroke and also to embark on my own project researching the story of Main Street, its buildings and the people who lived there.

I became one of the Society's leading members and helped

Sarah Haggar addresses a packed 'Haggar's Night' in Pembroke Town Hall.

organise a series of Haggar's Nights in Pembroke Town Hall which proved very successful – Pembroke people responded and we certainly played to a full houses!

The first of these was introduced by Roy's daughter, Sarah. Sarah gave an excellent presentation on the life and work of her great, great grandfather. She presented those travelling years of the Haggar family through the eyes of William's daughter Lily: the hardship, hunger and poverty.

Yet despite all this and against all the odds, William Haggar persevered with his moving pictures, strong in his conviction that 'there is money it'. Mark Jones composed a piano accompaniment to the silent movies so that the films could be viewed, as they were originally intended, to music. So many people commented afterwards that the music contributed so much to the experience and enjoyment of the films.

On a later occasion, we were fortunate to obtain the services of Sue Howley for another 'Night at the Silent Movies'. Sue is a brilliant pianist with an amazing ability to interpret the films in her music. She certainly breathed new life into them; the movies may have been silent but they were never meant to be viewed in silence. Accompanied by music, the experience was quite enthralling.

Sue, a musician/composer/teacher, was actually born in the Rhondda Valley which perhaps gives her that empathy with William Haggar and his films. This was a memorable night and, while the films were shown, everyone joined in with the action; laughing at the comedy and hissing and booing the villains. The films may have been made well over 100 years ago but they are still entertaining!

The Pembroke & Monkton Local History Society was also instrumental in organising Pembroke Museum which opened in June 2013. The Museum is a community project set up as a partnership between Pembroke Town Council (which provides the room) and heritage groups, including the West Wales Maritime Heritage Society and Pembroke Civic Trust.

It has all been done voluntarily - a museum for the community run by members of the community, raising their own money and relying on goodwill. As you will see from the next chapter, it is also home to an important Haggar archive.

Sarah Haggar with pianist Mark Jones.

Chapter 16
The films in Pembroke Museum

I WAS given responsibility for organising the Haggar collection in the Pembroke Museum which is now an important archive, bringing together written material, photographs, memorabilia and, above all, the remaining Haggar films which are available for all to see in the museum.

Although William Haggar is known to have made at least 60 films, only a few survive in their entirety today and we have copies of these for public viewing.

The films now showing in Pembroke Museum.

A Desperate Poaching Affray **(1903):**
Running time three minutes

FILMED in Maesteg in 1903, this complete film features Will Haggar Jnr., two of his brothers and actors from the Castle Theatre and was shot in just one afternoon. One of the first of the 'chase' films, *The Poachers* was very successful and sold around 480

'A Desperate Poaching Affray'.

copies including 100 which went to the USA. Notable for its non-stop action and innovative camera work, including the first ever panning shot, it is a real 'movie' rather than a filmed play.

The plot is a simple one. The poachers arrive on the scene and bag their prey but are surprised by gamekeepers and hide. As the gamekeepers and police search the bushes, the poachers make a dash for it and the chase is on.

The poachers fire on their police pursuers several times and the action includes river skirmishes, escapes and re-capture with passers by, even a pack of dogs, joining in the chase. The poachers are eventually captured and led away, totally dejected.

The Bathers' Revenge. (1904):
Running time: One minute.

TYPICAL of the 'Quickie', popular with the proprietors of fairground Bioscopes, this short comedy was shot one sunny afternoon on the Western Cleddau near Haverfordwest.

The 'lady' is Walter Haggar in drag and the bathers, local boys roped in for the occasion.

The film shows some young men enjoying a dip in the river having piled their clothes neatly on a seat on the riverbank. A courting couple enter the scene and, seeing the bathers' clothes

'The Bathers' Revenge'.

piled on the seat, throw them scornfully aside and sit down. The bathers take their revenge by grabbing the seat and toppling the amorous couple into the water.

With a tremendous show of leg kicking, splashing and vigorous contortion the couple manage to struggle out of the river watched by a very nonchalant big black dog.

Revenge! (1904):
Running time seven minutes.

THIS tale of injustice and revenge stars Will Jnr, thrown into an asylum by its villainous Master who seduces his wife. He escapes down a rope of knotted sheets (right) only to find his wife in the arms of the Master; in the ensuing struggle she is shot dead.

'Revenge!'

He is recaptured but again he escapes and, cornered on the edge of a precipice, he fights off his pursuers, four of whom fall to their deaths.

Having nothing left to live for, he returns to the asylum to exact his revenge by strangling the Master. This was considered to be one of Haggar's most violent films.

The Life of Charles Peace (1905):
Running time 13 minutes.

THIS film tells the story of the notorious Victorian burglar and murderer who was hanged in Armley Jail in Leeds in 1879 and is the oldest extant British story film.

Shot in and around Pembroke Dock, it stars Walter Haggar, playing the part of Charles Peace, with his mother, brothers Fred, Jim, Henry and sisters Lily and Violet all in the cast.

The film begins with Peace making attempts to seduce Mrs Dyson, then killing her husband. Discovered hiding under the bedclothes at his home, he is chased by police up onto the rooftops but manages to escape, changing his appearance by dressing in clerical garb and, his head held high with a sanctimonious expression on his face, handing out what would appear to be hymn sheets to the frustrated cops who throw them about in panic-stricken frustration.

Outwitting them, Peace appears centre screen looking quite calm but full of devilment and with a saucy look 'cocks a snook' in a full face close up into the camera before taking off at top speed leaving his pursuers behind.

However, Peace is eventually captured and, handcuffed with his head bowed, is escorted by police onto a train from which he attempts escape through a window. This effect was achieved with the use of a dummy representing Peace, who is then seen hobbling along the railway track, only to be recaptured.

The cowering Peace is picked out in an identity parade by Mrs Dyson, whom he then attacks, and is finally led to the scaffold, a noose around his neck and a bag over his head.

Two scenes from 'The Life of Charles Peace'.

A trap-door in the stage is released and Peace drops through it – quite strong stuff for a Victorian audience! William wanted to make this scene as realistic as possible and, although a soft landing stage was designed for Walter to land on, he had to fall quite a long way to achieve the reality of the scene. Consequently, he had rope burns around his neck and he always said that they nearly hanged him for real.

155

A Message from the Sea (1905):
Only a fragment of this film has survived.

HARRY Mainstay, a sailor played by Will Haggar Jnr. bids his parents goodbye at the gate of their cottage (right) and walks down to the Quay with his wife and children.

The remainder of the film is lost but the story involved a shipwreck and a desperate message in a bottle – 'shipwrecked, all alone on a raft, no hope God bless you, farewell' – committed to the sea by Harry and eventually received by his wife.

Assuming he was lost and all hope gone, his grieving wife, in her black widow's clothing, tends his memorial but then Harry, very much alive, surprises her. Her widow's hat is thrown aside and they embrace in a joyous finale.

The Stepney Wedding (1911):
Newsreel.

THIS is a fragment of a newsreel shot by William and Jim Haggar of a society wedding in Llanelli.

We see the wedding processions entering and leaving the church, shot from various angles. At the end of the film, one cameraman shoots the other: a rare opportunity of seeing William on film.

The Sheep Stealer (1908):
Running time eight minutes.

ANOTHER of Haggar's famous 'chase' films, *The Sheep Stealer* stars William's son Jim, his wife Kate and their two children.

'A Message from the Sea'.

Surviving in its entirety, this film was discovered in 2000 and tells the story of a husband forced into crime to feed his wife and two children.

The set reveals a family living in desperate poverty in a bare and empty cottage: once the film begins a large placard is displayed on screen with the words 'My wife and children

'The Stepney Wedding'.

'The Sheep Stealer'.

shall not starve'. The desperate husband searches for work and begs the farmer to employ him but, when his efforts fail, he steals a sheep in desperation, slings it over his shoulders and makes off with it.

The sheep stealer has chosen a very heavy animal – too heavy for him to carry far – and eventually it escapes when he can carry it no further. The shepherd, however, has informed the farmer and police who give chase with passers-by and their dogs joining in. The chase is seen to take place in open countryside and, as William Haggar enjoyed giving everyone a good soaking, across a weir eventually arriving back at his cottage where he is restrained by the farmer and the police.

At this point a second placard is displayed on screen with the words 'The Farmer forgives him'. Compassion has been shown and the farmer gives the family money.

The film ends with the happy family embracing.

The Maid of Cefn Ydfa (1914)
Running time 50 minutes, 38 minutes survive.

THE original *Maid of Cefn Ydfa*, made in 1902, literally made William Haggar's fortune and was one of the first British fictional films.

Filming conditions were primitive. No artificial lighting meant that films had to be shot in the open on a clear bright day: the timing of the shots was very much dependant on the elements. Ropes were placed at strategic points on the set to stop the actors straying out of the angle of vision of the camera and the film was shot in seven scenes in just over an hour. It ran for 15 minutes. There was a longer remake in 1908 which, like the original, has not survived.

This surviving film is the third version and lasted 50 minutes in its entirety; one of the longest British films of its day. Unfortunately, the film has partly disintegrated, but 38 minutes' worth survive in good condition and can still be enjoyed.

The film is based on an old Welsh folk tale and tells the love story of Ann Thomas, 'The Maid of Cefn Ydfa' and thatcher and poet, Will Hopcyn. The story was first adapted as a stage play in the 1870s, a popular Victorian melodrama and part of the Haggar repertoire.

The film was acted by Will Jnr.'s travelling theatre company and was filmed in Maesteg near Cefn Ydfa starring Will Jnr. as Will Hopcyn and his wife Jenny Lindon as Ann Thomas, the

Ann and Will in 'The Maid of Cefn Ydfa'.

Maid. The actor Will Fyffe (who may be better known for his 'I belong to Glasgow' fame) plays Lewis Bach, the comic relief; he was a member of the Haggar theatrical group for a considerable time.

The film begins with the cast parading at a local village festival in front of Will Hopcyn who is playing his harp. Will and

Ann meet and fall in love. However, social divisions at that time ensured that theirs was a union never to come to fruition and her mother schemes with the wealthy family solicitor to force Ann to marry his son, the obnoxious Anthony Maddocks.

After his proposal is rejected, Maddocks gets drunk at Bridgend Fair and assaults Ann which results in Will giving him a well-deserved thrashing. Ann is banned from seeing Will and, locked in her room and denied pen and paper to write to him, she writes a message on a leaf in her own blood.

However, she is duped into believing that Will has deserted her and marries Anthony, Will arriving at the church too late to prevent the wedding. He then really does go abroad but is pursued by Lewis Bach who intends to bring him home. The subtitle reads: 'Farewell England, Farewell Wales, I am off to the Rhondda Valley'.

Loss of Will, her unhappy marriage and the death of her child have driven Ann to distraction and the last scene shows her crying over the body of her dead baby. Ann removes her

Will arrives too late to prevent the wedding.

wedding ring, the subtitle declaring: 'It hurts like the sting of a snake – Will, Will, Why don't you come to me?'

The film ends here but, had it survived in its entirety, the audience would have seen Will returning to hold Ann in his arms where she dies.

Will Hopcyn was a musician and a bard; he wrote the Welsh folk song *Bugeilio'r Gwenith Gwyn* (Watching the White Wheat) in memory of his lost love.

I visited the village of Llangynwyd near Maesteg where the love story originated. The old mansion house 'Cefn Ydfa' no longer stands but the legend of 'The Maid of Cefn Ydfa' lives on in the village.

The little village pub, reputedly the oldest inn in South Wales, is fascinating with a great deal of information about the lovers displayed around the walls. We had a lovely meal there and afterwards went over to the churchyard to see the grave of Will Hopcyn who died in 1741. Ann Thomas died in 1727 but, being gentry, was buried inside the church.

Llangynwyd is a beautiful little village and I enjoyed my visit so much. I hope it was as pleasant for William Haggar and his production team when they made the film.

A distraught Ann at the grave of her dead baby.

William Haggar – Follow that Dream

WILLIAM Haggar was a man with a vision who overcame all the odds to see his dream come to fruition: a true pioneer whose success was so well deserved.

But this success did not end with William; the talents of the actor, musician, stage manager, showman, movie maker, cinema proprietor, entrepreneur and family man were carried through the next four generations in his children, his grand children and great grand children.

Sadly, Haggars Cinema in Pembroke was the very last Haggar family cinema and the end of an era, although not the end of the story.

As I finish the closing chapter of this book, I know that the memory of the Haggars will continue, never to be forgotten, especially in Pembroke.